The Kindness Effect

The Kindness Effect

JILL DONOVAN

CHARISMA
HOUSE

Most CHARISMA HOUSE BOOK GROUP products are available at special quantity discounts for bulk purchase for sales promotions, premiums, fund-raising, and educational needs. For details, write Charisma House Book Group, 600 Rinehart Road, Lake Mary, Florida 32746, or telephone (407) 333-0600.

THE KINDNESS EFFECT by Jill Donovan
Published by Charisma House
Charisma Media/Charisma House Book Group
600 Rinehart Road
Lake Mary, Florida 32746
www.charismahouse.com

Cover design by Justin Evans

Visit the author's website at rusticcuff.com.

Library of Congress Control Number: 2018932067
International Standard Book Number: 978-1-62999-179-5
E-book ISBN: 978-1-62999-180-1

While the author has made every effort to provide accurate internet addresses at the time of publication, neither the publisher nor the author assumes any responsibility for errors or for changes that occur after publication. Further, the publisher does not have any control over and does not assume any responsibility for author or third-party websites or their content.

18 19 20 21 22 — 9 8 7 6 5 4 3
Printed in the United States of America

To Terry, Ireland, and Peanut.
You and my heart are one and the same.

There is my heart,
and then there is you,
and I'm not sure there is a difference.[1]
—A. R. ASHER

CONTENTS

Part III
Speaking Off the Cuff

ACKNOWLEDGMENTS

S PECIAL THANKS TO Tessie DeVore—I am almost certain, without your persistence, gentle prodding, and humor, this book would never have even begun.

Thank you to my editors Debbie Marrie and Melissa Bogdany not only for pouring hours, weeks, and months into editing but also for having an abundant amount of grace for the missed deadlines.

To Erin Bates for daily reminding me this journey was possible and reminding me to just take it one day at a time. Your help was invaluable and turned my impossibility into reality. Thank you for that.

To Jordan Coffman, Robyn Peck, Kacy Griesemer, Daniele Bushong, and Erika Hester for the extremely memorable moments (mostly because of your combined sharp wit) when it came to naming the book. That is a text thread I will forever cherish.

To Meagen Smith not only for being there every day for over half a decade now but for being the great coordinator of all things for my life.

To Matt Griffin for the time you spent reading the book over and over again when you didn't even have time to read your own book for your book club. But mostly for being the model of kindness to every person you meet.

Thank you to my mom, Judy Reamer.

Actually, this thank-you should be in all caps.

So THANK YOU, Mom! To say I don't know how this book

could have been completed without you is an extreme understatement. Not only are you an amazing writer yourself, but your eye for editing and the way you put everything aside to help me regardless of what else was going on are why you are the mom I aspire to be.

To Pat McCauley and Sandy Feit not only for allowing my mom to convince you that this was the editing project for you but for working on it as if it were your own book.

To Bo Wright, Daniele Bushong, and Jessica Bushong for making the book come to life through the best book trailer I have ever watched.

To Kevin and Tonya Anderson for all of your help and creativity in discussing the book cover. Those were some of my favorite memories of this entire process. It didn't hurt that we were in the snowy mountains of Utah at the time!

To Amy Impellizzeri. You are an inspiration to all who want to step outside of their box and go for it. You went for it. And I am your biggest fan.

To Suzy Graham. We all need someone who shows us that the mountain is not as big as it seems. You are that person for me. How did I survive the first four decades of my life without you?

And finally, to Terry and the girls for allowing me the freedom to write and giving your unconditional love and joy every step of the way.

FOREWORD

When Jill Donovan picked me up from the airport in Tulsa, Oklahoma, in September 2016, I had no idea I had just met a kindred spirit. It didn't take long for us to hit it off as she drove me to the Gold Medal Gala, a fund-raiser for a nonprofit gymnastics program called Aim High Academy.

I had been invited to be the keynote speaker at the fund-raiser, and Jill was my host, which meant she drove me to and from the airport and made sure I had everything I needed in between. We made an instant connection and chatted as if we'd known each other for years. I learned of her lifelong love of gymnastics and that even though it never did become her career, it was the catalyst that inspired her to continue learning and searching for other things she was passionate about.

Jill also told me I inspired her as a young gymnast to push past the pain and to dream bigger dreams, but in truth I was simply just blessed by God in my life, and that's my message to everyone I meet. I was told I'd never make it to the Olympics, but with God's help and hard work I persevered.

That's the culture of gymnastics—we don't stop; we don't give up when people tell us no. When we lose something, we determine we will gain it back again. That's a big part of my story, and I learned it's a big part of Jill's story as well.

Her hospitality and enthusiasm throughout my trip to Tulsa were infectious. So it's no surprise to me that she's written *The Kindness Effect*, a book full of real-life stories exemplifying what can happen when you discover your gifts and become intentional about using them.

That's exactly what Jill did. She left the legal profession when she followed her heart and discovered her true passion for giving. The result was the foundation of her wildly popular Rustic Cuff business. Now her favorite thing to do is inspire a giving heart in others. For Jill, it's not about the gift itself but the connection made between two people.

As you read *The Kindness Effect*, you'll savor every page of Jill's engaging, honest, witty personality, and, like me, you'll feel as if you've made a new best friend. Jill is not afraid to laugh at herself or reveal her innermost thoughts as she invites you to share her most embarrassing moments, deepest sorrows, and greatest joys. Through it all she weaves poignant lessons she's learned about the power of generous giving for a fulfilled journey through life.

After I spoke at that Aim High fund-raiser in Tulsa, Jill performed a floor routine in a celebrity gymnastic competition, and I was the judge, which was a lot of fun. Watching her perform, I could almost see the nine-year-old who dreamed those Olympic-sized dreams. Although her path led her elsewhere, I could still see the trademark characteristic of determination and drive that many gymnasts, athletes, and other successful people share.

When I give motivational talks like the one I gave in Tulsa that day, I tell kids they can achieve anything if they believe in it and commit to it with their whole heart. Through the pages of this book you'll discover that during those times when Jill faced adversity and setbacks, she found a way to use them for good. By believing in herself and following her "knower" (something she'll explain to you as you read further), she took what could have been the most devastating moment in her life and turned it into the greatest accomplishment. That's what I've come to admire about her, and I know it's what inspires everyone she meets.

I'm often quoted as saying, "Each of us has a fire in our heart for something, and it's our goal in life to find it and keep it lit." I believe the quote became popular because so many of us understand what it feels like to search for our purpose and the indescribable joy that comes with finding it. As you read *The Kindness Effect*, I know you'll come to agree with me that Jill's journey from nine-year-old aspiring gymnast to CEO of Rustic Cuff has been one of a burning heart, and it's why she is so enthusiastic about igniting the flame of passion and purpose in others. The true stories Jill shares in this book will inspire you to discover your talent, gift, skill, or passion and use it to benefit others. She has lived out this message with amazing results, and she wants you to know that you can too.

—MARY LOU RETTON
AUTHOR, SPEAKER, AND OLYMPIC GOLD MEDALIST

THE *NEVER* LIST

N EARLY SIX YEARS ago, while on sabbatical from teaching law at the University of Tulsa (Oklahoma), I took time to reflect on my future. More specifically I wanted to discover my passion. To help compartmentalize each idea that came to me, I made two lists. The first one was to itemize some good choices for the years ahead. The other was my *never* list. It was definitive!

> I *never* want to be an entrepreneur. (There's too much work involved.)

> I *never* want to have employees. (I already have a family.)

> I *never* want to write a book (even though I love to read).

Notice the last item? Yet here you are holding a volume written by a once very reluctant author. My publisher had some major convincing on its hands trying to obtain an agreement from me to write a book. The first time they contacted me, my answer was simply, "It's a firm *no*." Furthermore, to do some major convincing on my end, I emailed the publisher my *never* list. The font size for "I *never* want to write a book" was much larger than that of the first two items. I might even have changed the text color to make those words light up the page!

Six months later I was on the phone with the publisher a second time. The publisher was asking if a change of mind was possible. I wasn't as bold this time, but the answer was still *no*. (To my surprise, the tenor of my voice was a bit softer than in my initial reply.)

Realizing something had changed in me, I knew I should listen to my "knower." (I use that term to reference following my heart, listening to the small voice within, being sensitive to promptings, discerning situations, etc.) There was a little spark in my "knower," and I thought, "Maybe I just need to peek around this corner to see what it's all about." (I was inspired, at this point, to turn my firm *no* into a quiet *yes*.)

An aside: I have started to accomplish, much to my astonishment, many things I had previously determined *never* to do! Here's the secret: outsmart the list by playing the opposite game!

So now my new *never* list reads:

I will *never* be in shape.

I will *never* have the house organized.

I will *never* have all the laundry done.

I will *never* get my children to eat vegetables.

This book is not a how-to guide on exercising kindness. It is also not the story of my business, Rustic Cuff. It would only be the size of a booklet at best if that had been all I'd chosen to pen. Instead, you'll read a compilation of stories exemplifying what might happen if we respond to opportunities for joy that irrational giving can bring.

The takeaway from these stories, and many others like them, is that every person has a talent, gift, skill, or passion that can be used to benefit others. We are all different, and our abilities and resources are different too, but that doesn't matter. Discovering what our particular gifts are and purposely using them to bless others is the reason we have gifts in the first place.

For example, do you love to cook? You can take a meal to someone who is sick. Do you enjoy the elderly? You can visit the lonely in a nursing home since there are many who have no visitors. Are you an encourager, a gardener, or an organizer? The list of gifts is long, but anything we have that is given in kindness and done from the heart will bring joy to the receiver and to us, the givers.

When you read these pages, some chapters may completely resonate with you, and others will have you thinking, "This story only happens to other people." I've either witnessed or personally experienced each of these stories, which make up a life I never knew I wanted. There may be a chapter here or there that doesn't relate to anything you are experiencing now or have ever tasted in the past. Yet I believe other chapters will grab you, almost as if you're looking in a mirror.

As you go through different seasons of life, you may find yourself facing a detour that points to the right when you thought the next turn would absolutely be to the left. It's bad enough that you're being rerouted, but then come potholes! Can you relate?

No matter where you are now, or where you land in your unfolding future, you will most likely see glimmers of your reflection in most of the chapters. I hope this book will be a support for you and enable you to embrace your journey, whatever the hazards.

I've read many books over the years, and there are a handful I choose to revisit when I need a little extra wisdom, encouragement, and humor. My hope is that *The Kindness Effect* will become that for you.

PART I
PURSUE YOUR PASSION—
THEREIN LIES YOUR CALLING

*Hardships often prepare ordinary people
for an extraordinary destiny.*
—UNKNOWN

Chapter 1

WHAT FEELS LIKE THE END IS OFTEN THE BEGINNING

I BELIEVED I WAS meant to be a gymnast. From the age of nine, going for the gold medal was always in the forefront of my mind. Nadia Comaneci and Olga Korbut kept the dream alive by smiling at me daily from my bedroom wall. I believed there would someday be a big poster of me hanging on my wall next to theirs and the three of us would be exchanging triumphant smiles!

My training schedule was rigorous. You'd find me practicing at the gym four afternoons a week after school, in addition to countless hours spent practicing outside of the gym. I practiced my roundoff in school hallways when no one was looking. And whenever I was watching innocuous TV shows at home, you'd catch me sitting in a butterfly stretch position to help my splits.

I dreamed about winning and could almost hear the crowd roaring as I completed each gymnastic move. In my dream I could audibly hear my heart beating followed by great relief as I finished at the top of each event. No amount of practice, no amount of time required, and no pain was too great to keep me from persevering. I was determined to compete in the Olympics.

Having been selected for the competitive gymnastic team, after my first and only tryout, solidified the idea I was on the path, one step closer to my ultimate dream. I lived, breathed, and loved everything that had to do with my passion. This was true even on the most frustrating days of polishing my routines.

Then came a rude awakening in the form of crushing news. I call it rude because at the time, it felt plain rude! The devastating news came on the heels of a grueling practice while I was packing my gym bag. My coach, Eric, pulled me to the side. "Jill, I am going to level with you." (Ever the optimist, I was sure he was going to promote me to the next team level.) He went on, "Someone needs to tell you the truth before you continue to spend more time and money on something in which you have no future."

Have you ever had a moment in time so life changing that you remember your outfit and who was standing around? In my case, I recall experiencing tunnel vision, with a low hum in my head. I can still feel the raw emotions as if it were yesterday. It was 1979, a Thursday afternoon.

At first I couldn't hear Eric's words. It was as if he were talking through the ever-fuzzy intercom at school. The coach stopped and asked if I was listening. I swallowed back my tears and nodded yes. He went on to say, "You simply do not have what it takes to make it to a higher-level team. Your flexibility and techniques have recently plateaued, and I just haven't seen the type of improvement I need to see at this stage. I do not see the possibility of the necessary improvement at this point." He ended our chat with a pat on my back, a smile, and a suggestion: "Consider excelling in another activity that may help when applying for a college scholarship down the road. It's never too soon to think about that."

College? I was stunned when he used that word. I was going straight to the Olympics. My mind was racing. I knew all of this was just a big misunderstanding. My thoughts were: "OK, so technique and flexibility are my weak points. Aren't there flexibility vitamins I can take to help? That seems logical. Or maybe he really meant to have this conversation with Julie. He probably mixed us up because we both have short hair and our names start with a J. And no future, he said? Did I hear him correctly? Wait just a minute, Eric. There is no way you are squashing my dream right here, right now."

After my heartbeat slowed and the tunnel vision cleared, I understood Eric was thinking of me, not Julie. I tried to digest what he had said. It felt as if I'd received a punch in the stomach. I left the gym that day thinking this man had crushed my dreams.

It took a while for me to get over the initial heartbreak and to accept the kindly given truth—I was not meant to be an Olympic gymnast. I resolved that if I couldn't be an Olympian, then I'd attempt to do something different, new, and exciting every single year. Each January my plan was to choose a novel activity to fully engage in for the next twelve months. I promised myself I'd jump on my new hobbyhorse and ride it for all it's worth and never jump off to ask myself, "What if I fail?"

> **It felt as if I'd received a punch in the stomach. I left the gym that day thinking this man had crushed my dreams.**

Though each new passion might not turn out to be my life's calling, at least I would give it a chance. Most likely no awards would come my way. In addition, my interest in the "hobby" could possibly wane by year's end, but during that year I'd commit to giving my all to the one new venture.

I figured if I kept this plan going until age forty, there'd be some thirty new skills in my life's portfolio. (Yes, I did the math.) The idea of owning a new talent each year was heartening and fun for my almost ten-year-old mind. "Jill-of-all-trades"—my new dream.

Chapter 2

JILL-OF-ALL-TRADES, MASTER OF NONE

WITH MY NEWFOUND determination to be the "Jill-of-all-trades"—instead of the master of one—I picked a brand-new hobby to pursue the first of January. Then, at the end of every year, I would gather my friends and family to watch some sort of performance showcasing the twelve months' acquired skill.

Once I recovered from the loss of my gymnastic dream, it was as if my entire world opened up to endless possibilities. The mere idea I could learn a new skill every year instead of focusing on just one thing created a great enthusiasm to begin right away.

"Thank you, Eric." I quietly voiced those words at the start of each new year. It was born out of gratitude for my treasured coach's honesty, even though he knew it would hurt his aspiring gold medalist. I'd still be in the gym today working to master the splits had it not been for Eric's gifting me with a ticket to experience new interests—ones that were part and parcel of a pursuit to find my ultimate passion. In hindsight I see how an ordinary Thursday afternoon in 1979 was turned into a life-changing day.

As the years passed, my list of new skills and hobbies grew. For example, one year I took up photography, another year the violin, another year art lessons. Adding layer upon layer of hobbies has afforded me a rich education and fun-filled months of learning.

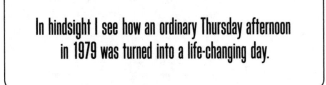

In hindsight I see how an ordinary Thursday afternoon in 1979 was turned into a life-changing day.

For example, the year I decided to study a formidable language is quite memorable. I wanted to fluently speak a language nobody else in school was studying—Russian. For what purpose? At that point I wasn't sure, but I gave it my all. Every piece of furniture and every object in my home had a sticker on it with its Russian name. I went on to study the difficult language in college and spent a summer in Russia after I graduated. This was one of the highlights of my life. I had no idea the quest to be well-rounded would lead to wonderful relationships with some Russians—ones with whom I was able to communicate on a deep level.

Never to be forgotten were the twelve delightful months spent living in the world of…harmonica. I was in my early twenties when I made my first visit to a music store, and I walked out with two harmonicas and a music book. I practiced making music daily on this tiny apparatus. Before long I was playing a variety of songs.

I even was playing on two different harmonicas! Don't be too impressed. I played them the same way, but one was in the key of C, and one in the key of D. My purse carried both in case I got the urge to break out musically.

The "harmonica year" flew by so quickly that before I knew it, Christmas was a week away. I hadn't yet organized my recital. With the holidays right around the corner, there was no viable way to plan a performance and expect people to show up before the new year started. I always had to have some sort of closure for each year's hobby. What's a girl to do? This year I would be forced to push back on my superstition that a concert must take place before the new year began. Not easy for me...

During Christmas week I was on a Southwest Airlines flight to visit family. The seating was on a first-come-first-serve basis. Only a few seats were left by the time I boarded. There was one seat in the front row and two middle seats further back. In the nineties on Southwest the front row faced backward. Perhaps this seat was available because no one wanted other travelers looking their way for a long time. Who would want that seat? Aha! The thought came: "Hold on just a second. *I* would! I want people staring at me! Not for hours on end but for a long enough time to conduct a small recital!"

I laughed to myself as I sat down in the backward-facing seat. God has a wonderful sense of humor. He must have created that backward row just for me to sit in—*for that day, for that moment, for the specific purpose of giving a harmonica concert midair.*

Problem: I wanted the entire plane to hear what I had learned during the previous eleven months, but how would they all be able to hear me? Engine noise would be an issue, so I prayed for this to be a quieter-than-usual flight. And suddenly, as if God and Southwest Airlines had heard my prayer, there was a change in plans as we pushed off from the gate. The pilot's voice came over the loudspeaker: "This is your captain speaking. So sorry, ladies and gentlemen. Due to inclement weather we've been advised of a delay. We will be on the tarmac for an hour before takeoff."

You could hear the moaning and groaning. The mere thought of sitting on the tarmac for that long made for a vast number of agitated and disappointed fliers. Hold on just a minute, though... What if I could lift their spirits with something they hadn't bargained for—free entertainment! It just so happens I may be able to lend a helping hand, in the form of a Christmas harmonica recital.

I know that most people would be frustrated, sorely irritated, with *any* delay but especially a delay on a tarmac in a packed airplane. I gave no thought to these minor details. This recital was going to be better than I could've imagined. The delay meant not only that I would have the entire plane's attention for a solid hour, but it would also be quiet enough to hear my songs, even in the bathroom. Why's that? The engines would not be running.

> I've heard it said, "If you haven't caused it and can't control it, then you can't cure it." What a help that truth can be in our daily lives.

I quickly pulled out the key of C harmonica, took a deep breath, and went for it. This was the moment I had been preparing for all year long and had no idea would be played out this way. In front of approximately 130 passengers I was able to play every single Christmas carol I could think of. Some of them I played twice. Okay—maybe three times. I even took requests.

I realize it sounds absurd and foolish to play a harmonica on an airplane full of disgruntled passengers. But something wonderful happened that morning as I saw their stress dissipating. Just the simplicity of a harmonica and some Christmas carols brought a bit of relief to an otherwise inconvenient situation. I've heard it said, "If you haven't caused it and can't control it, then you can't cure it." What a help that truth can be in our daily lives. But in this situation, though I hadn't caused it and I couldn't control it, I was glad to offer, in a small way, a musical "cure."

I found real joy in playing the harmonica for the passengers, but not because there was a rationale to pursue a music career and join a band (but don't count me out yet). Nor was it because I gave a perfect concert to a perfect audience. The joy in my heart was simply because a little bit of magic happened that morning.

Thank you, Eric.

That same kind of magic happens every December after I've spent the year developing a new skill. And so, with the recital on the airplane concluding the "year of the harmonica," I tapped into a new experience—*dancing*, specifically tap dancing.

One early January day I began taking private tap lessons. Loved every minute of it! I grew up watching old movies starring legendary tap dancers Ginger Rogers and Fred Astaire, so I secretly wished someday, somehow, my feet would learn to move just like theirs. I couldn't believe I'd not yet thought of tap dancing as a new skill to take on.

The weekly class was taught by seventy-year-old Fay, who could outdance just about anyone I knew at the time. She was passionate about tap dancing, having won more awards than she knew what to do with. I soaked up everything I could, and after many weeks of challenging work I asked about Fay's annual recital. This would involve her entire dancing school. "The recital will take place at an auditorium in a local high school," Fay answered. "I've picked out your costume design, and we're going to have it made. It's gorgeous!"

I planned accordingly:

- Location—check!

- Costume—check!

- Recital music—check!

- Oral invitations to friends and family—check!

"Jill, there will be three other students who are learning your same routine. The four of you will perform together onstage."

I was happy to reply, "This is going to be more fun than I can imagine!"

Thinking about meeting these other women, who must also be private students, I hoped for lunch together at some point, trusting we'd become fast friends. Our teamwork onstage should knit us together well. We'd be braving a recital mostly filled with little ones and teens ranging from three to fourteen years old.

I asked Fay when we four would practice together, and to my surprise she told me there was little need since we were all doing well individually. She had a "good feeling" everything would come together at our dress rehearsal. I concluded Fay didn't want me to meet the others too far in advance since one (or more) may have been a far better "tapper" than I was. My thoughtful tutor was most likely concerned I'd be intimidated—she probably feared, "Oh, no! Jill might suddenly 'come down with the flu' on recital night."

I was pretty relaxed the night of the dress rehearsal. I knew the routine well, and it helped that the audience that afternoon wouldn't unnerve me too much since the turnout—a few parents and friends—would be small. The dancers were given separate times to arrive for rehearsal, so not many would be there for any one routine.

Wearing my costume, I left the dressing room and saw three other people wearing similar sparkly outfits. I didn't give it much thought. Heading to the auditorium, the four of us wound up walking single file down the hall, with me as the caboose. On the way I had this puzzling thought: "These are my fellow performers who just happen to be nearly twenty years younger than I am!" William was eight years old, and the two girls, Morgan and Nicole, were five-year-olds. I was the odd man out, being the only one over the age of ten.

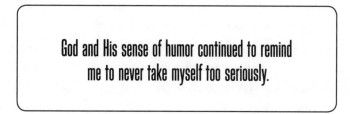

God and His sense of humor continued to remind me to never take myself too seriously.

Asking Fay the ages of the other dancers had never occurred to me. I suddenly wanted to run ("Maybe I'll sprain an ankle!") but opted for a wiser choice. I'd embrace the moment with..."Whatever." My usual perspective concerning life replaced the thoughts urging me to take flight. I realized it was not by chance that William, Morgan, Nicole, and I were going to be dancing partners. I decided to just roll with it and embrace it fully—half laughing, half embarrassed.

The recital the following night went as planned, but I knew full well who did the planning. God and His sense of humor continued to remind me to never take myself too seriously. I recall laughing so hard after the recital that my stomach muscles were sore the next day. The three little ones were over-the-top cute in their costumes and tap-danced their young hearts out. I imagined us looking like ducklings walking toward the stage that night, in single file, all in the same costume, but age and gender appropriate, of course. I had to keep from laughing out loud while tapping my own little heart out—mama alongside her little ducklings. At least I had all my ducks in a row.

You'd have thought my tap-dancing experience would slow my desire to continue pursuing hobbies, but not even that could deter me. After all, I still hadn't given ice-skating a try! One of my favorite childhood memories was watching the Winter Olympic Games with my mom. Figure skating was one of our favorite events, especially when Jayne Torvill and Christopher Dean performed. I was fascinated with each turn, spin, and jump. Awestruck, with my eyes glued to the screen, I could almost feel the intensity of the skating pair. I held my breath watching these favorites perform their hardest routines.

With those vivid memories in mind, I decided to dedicate a year to learning how to figure-skate. The journey began when I woke up on a beautiful Saturday morning. Outside the sun shone, the air was cool and crisp, and the ground was covered with a light layer of snow. What a perfect day to get out and find the perfect pair of ice skates. I wanted them to be shiny and bright white, like the weather...and like I believed the year ahead would be.

It turned out to be an easy shopping day since I found the perfect pair right away. Later I signed up for lessons and met my trainer at the gigantic rink. He was astonished to hear I wanted to become an excellent figure skater in one year—especially when I made my confession: "I've only been on the ice twice. One time was at Rockefeller Center in Manhattan, and I was on the ground more than I was skating."

My trainer, however, decided he was up for the challenge, and we started my training the following Monday. I was not prepared for the difficulty of the movements—well, that's the very definition of a gross understatement. The ice skaters I had watched my entire life made gliding across the ice look quite effortless. I, on the other hand, struggled to stay upright for more than sixty seconds.

As I noticed each passing year, the end of December always seemed to arrive in record speed. For this figure-skating closure I would be performing a solo routine in a competition, rather than being part of a recital. Even months before the competition I was excited just thinking about the upcoming performance. I had the perfect costume, my still perfectly shiny white ice skates, and, even more importantly, I had the perfect song as background music— Whitney Houston's song "I Believe in You and Me." What an amazing voice she had!

The competition day arrived. I was a nervous wreck thinking about presenting my routine. My anxiety was so high, I might as well have been competing in the Olympics. I had just learned my toughest variation, called the Biellmann spin, in which I lifted one leg behind me and held my toe toward my head. I was afraid I wouldn't be able to pull off that move since it was very new to me. Add to that, I was afraid my intricate choreography would be forgotten, even though I had gone over and over each move a million times in my head that morning.

I was the last skater to compete in my age category. Up in the stands a crowd of young moms and dads had been cheering for their children, which made me more anxious. At this point my friends were used to the annual invitation to my end-of-the-year hobby recital. I had a couple dozen of my friends and family members show up, so I definitely felt supported. However, I still wanted to make this announcement: "My name is Jill. This is my first competition. The routine I have prepared for you will be best experienced if you simply close your eyes and sway to the music."

Deciding—as I had done with other hobbies—to embrace the

task, I gave it 100 percent. There was no reason in only giving it 50 percent. What would be the point of that? The next thing I knew, my truly sweet and encouraging trainer was standing by me. "You're up! Let's go! You can do this!" I was now afraid of disappointing him, which added to the other anxieties.

Remarkably, the moment I heard Whitney Houston through the speakers and the instant my skates hit the ice, I blocked everything else out and found the courage to tell myself, "This is just like any other normal practice day." Those words reaped a great reward.

I skated the routine and felt this was the best I'd done all year. I even nailed the Biellmann position that had me so worried. I recollected an ordinary Thursday in 1979 when my gymnastics coach told me I would never be flexible enough to accomplish such skills. If only he could see me now. I had given a gold-medal-worthy performance, even if the gold medal was made of plastic.

> I finally was beginning to see the purpose for the pain of a dream that was dashed many years ago . . . the purpose of an expanded horizon filled with new knowledge, abundant joy, and treasured moments I might have otherwise missed.

Next up was the awards ceremony for my age category. I was still beaming with pride. Apparently the judges liked my performance as well because I heard my name announced for the gold medal. I could not believe my ears! As I walked toward the podium to receive my medal, I imagined flowers being thrown on the rink in celebration. Suddenly, as I stood on the first-place podium, the dais seemed to get smaller. Come to find out, there were only two competitors in my age group, and the judges decided we should share the first-place award. And there we were, the two champions trying not to fall off the small platform...all the while posing for pictures.

Though I may not have become the third member of Torvill and Dean, I did gain from that experience as well as from every other hobby before and after that year. What I learned was more valuable than any medal, award, or title I could receive. I learned no challenge was too big to face. The bigger the challenge, the more rewarding the outcome.

I finally was beginning to see the purpose for the pain of a dream that was dashed in 1979—the purpose being an expanded horizon filled with new knowledge, abundant joy, and treasured moments I might have otherwise missed. The road was making a curve to the right when all along I thought it was supposed to go left.

Thank you, Eric.

Thank You, God.

Chapter 3

THE ART OF REGIFTING

A FTER HIGH SCHOOL I received a soccer scholarship and landed in Oklahoma, where I faced four years of fun, fun, fun, and study—or, more appropriately, study, study, study, and fun...and of course soccer. I graduated with a degree in organization/interpersonal communication and a minor in business. My first job after graduation was with MetLife, and then I was hired by American Airlines, where I was aiming to captain a Boeing 757. OK, that last part is a stretch...yet I did enjoy the benefits of working for an airline.

While at American Airlines I began to consider making a final career choice. I wanted to have a one-word titled profession. I provided myself with three options:

- A doctor
- An accountant
- An attorney

Which choice might be the most fulfilling? I wondered, "What would life as Dr. Jill Reamer look like?" I don't much care for blood or needles. And for sure I never want to be responsible for such important things as body parts! Therefore becoming a doctor was out.

The next option was to become a CPA. I recalled my college accounting classes. Suddenly the thought came, "I could have used a tutor at the time." Although I was a business minor, I'd made a mental note that balance sheets should be handled by those who know what they are doing. Furthermore, two of my brothers, both bright, were already accountants, and another, bright also, graduated with a finance and business degree. Four of us juggling numbers? Not a promising idea. I had reached my *numbers* limit playing Monopoly with the three of them. Strike through *accountant*.

An attorney? Was that to be my path? My dad was an attorney, and my grandfather a judge, so it seemed as if practicing law might be a natural fit. And it also took care of the "one word" prerequisite. Check.

I began to imagine graduating from law school and passing the bar exam. "Could I do it? Should I do it?" These were the exact questions that ran through my mind before I began any new hobby. Starting as a ten-year-old, by the end of each year I had moved a bit further in overcoming the fear of failure. The combination of all the past years brought me closer to the moment of decision. One more thing helped move me forward with a law school application: I could be both doctor and lawyer! Two of my career options could be realized. I imagined the sign on my office door: JILL REAMER, JURIS DOCTOR.

With great excitement and unlimited possibilities for my future, I enrolled in law school. It would be a huge challenge, but I once again wanted to jump in with both feet and give it my all.

After completing my first year of law school, I married Terry Donovan, a one-in-a-million man. How I appreciated the audience of one, who was always available for a solo harmonica concert. My year of art lessons came into play when I discovered Terry had artistic talent. The two of us sat together, with brushes, oils, and acrylics in hand, happily painting on large canvases. Though tap dancing was part of my repertoire, that fun activity never became part of Terry's. He would have smiled and politely declined at the mere suggestion.

After two years in law school, I felt this profession wasn't a life-long dream or a passion of the heart. I'd listen to my professors talk about the law and what could be done with a degree, and I never quite landed on "This really stirs my soul." I knew, however, getting a law degree could be extremely beneficial in other ways. Yet I was never certain this was what I was *called* to do.

One afternoon while studying property law, I took a short break and turned on the television. I started watching *The Oprah Winfrey Show*. I had met someone the previous year who had been in the audience of the show and had described the experience in detail. It was during that year I began my quest to get tickets to be in the audience during one of Oprah's tapings. I had grown up watching her, and I knew this was something I wanted to do before she retired. My pursuit for the tickets became *my new hobby*.

Nothing more.

Nothing less.

For as long as I could remember, I had watched almost every episode, as I was fascinated with the stories people would tell and how Oprah was able to draw out every emotion from all walks of life.

I made it my mission to simply call once a day for tickets. And by *mission* I mean that is exactly what it became—a *mission*. My new hobby for the year! The more I was told that there were no tickets available, the more determined I was to find them. At this point standing in an overflow room, watching the show on a small television in the same building would have satisfied me. Day after day I tried, never giving up. The perseverance continued as I tackled thick, heavy law books to get my degree.

> I began to equate work with unfulfillment and a heaviness that never quite lifted.

Before I knew it, I had graduated, passed the bar exam, and started working as a lawyer. Most can't wait to get out of school so they can start practicing law. But I was the opposite, having loved every aspect of law school. The reading, the courses, the discussions, the debates—I loved it all. Did I mention reading? Lots and lots and lots of reading. I might even go so far as to say I could have stayed in school forever. Well, maybe.

What I didn't love was what came afterward—meaning the actual work that comes with being an attorney. I never tasted the passion I was searching for, especially since I was working as a family law/divorce attorney. Other than the satisfaction of advocating for others and helping them go through very difficult times, I found little joy when dealing with clients going through a divorce. The best way to describe it: you are helping, at times, some great people going through one of the worst times of their lives. My Pollyanna attitude had an awkward time staying afloat some days. After a while the days seemed to run together. I found myself wasting away perfectly good Sundays at home, anxiously dreading the upcoming workweek. I began to equate work with unfulfillment and a heaviness that never quite lifted.

Through it all my quest to be in the audience of *The Oprah Winfrey Show* continued. By this point it had been five years of trying. My twelve-month challenge had stretched out a wee bit! The ticket office phone number was on redial. I only had to push one button to call. I kept the speakerphone volume down very low, not wanting my constant phone calls to be overheard in the law office. Should I have known how problematic it was to get tickets? There was a busy signal nearly every time I called. Apparently most people were going through the same wait. If by chance my call did go through, I was told that no tickets were available anytime soon. Nevertheless I was determined to get closure, and there was only one way to do it—get those tickets.

This Russian-speaking, tap-dancing, harmonica-playing girl, who could also figure-skate, play the violin, and do the balance beam, was determined to have this new experience. A bonus perk meant traveling to Chicago and a much-needed vacation with Terry to one of my favorite cities.

One afternoon during my fifth year of trying to get tickets, I finished a meeting with one of my clients and sat down at my desk with a renewed determination to get closure. On this day I pulled up the show's website to see if there was something I missed in the hunt to secure seats. The opening screen came up, and in big, bold letters, as if it were written just for me, was "Be on the show!"

"What? Be on the show? Of course I would like to be on the show! How was this something I had never thought of before?"

This was potentially my back door to finally getting closure. It was as if a bright neon sign were blinking and calling my name. I couldn't believe I hadn't thought of this earlier. I clicked on the link, and a page came up: "Do any of these topics in the following list sound like you? Tell us your story. We want to hear." I prayed there'd be a topic that resonated with some aspect of my life.

I squinted, afraid to see the screen, and then I read the first sentence: "Are you a regifter?"

"Am I a regifter? I absolutely am a regifter!"

I was practically born and raised a regifter! It felt as if they were talking directly to me.

All the thanks go to my loving mom. She is a conference speaker and very often finds beautiful baskets in her hotel rooms filled with gifts. A basket from an inviting group served to welcome its speaker. My mom would arrive home with scented candles, pot holders, picture frames, doilies, mints, scarves, boxes of note cards, pens, cheeses, plaques, warm socks, perfumes, handkerchiefs, tiny flashlights, sunglasses, books, a mug imprinted with Niagara Falls, a map of highspots in Texas, and more. Once a group included a framed picture of Elvis—she was in Mississippi.

All these items were good feed for her gift closet. Mom never made it home, though, with the dark chocolates or Snickers. Sadly never did she arrive home with a cute puppy for her four adorable children or with caviar for Dad.

My mom had the idea that instead of going shopping when we needed a gift for a friend, her children could just grab something from the gift closet. There's just a small detail to factor in about this closet—the gifts. They were from the *hotel* baskets, and some were from a wide circle of friends...or her mother-in-law. She believed the presents could be put to better use in someone else's home.

Given that my mom is two or three decades older than my brothers and me, our choices of gifts were somewhat...limited. Not exactly age appropriate. As you can imagine, my three brothers and I experienced some awkward moments at birthday parties when our gifts were opened.

> My mom had the idea that instead of going shopping when we needed a gift for a friend, her children could just grab something from the gift closet.

Once, when I was nine years old, I needed a gift for a birthday party. Like most children, I wanted to go to the huge TG&Y store to pick out the newest and most fun toy in the place. Instead, I was staring in the gift closet, wondering if the birthday girl, who was also turning nine that day, would rather have a scented candle, a plaque inscribed with "Expect a Miracle," or an audiocassette titled *How to Have a Better Marriage*. I went with the candle and tried to act thrilled when she opened my gift. I figured no one would notice how inappropriate my gift was if I acted as if it were the best thing invented. At the very least, my excitement might distract from the gift I gave. There were never any duplicates of what I brought. That was nice.

When I was fifteen years old, while in the middle of looking through the closet for yet another half-appropriate gift that would cause me the least embarrassment possible, I came to a decision. I am finished with "gift closeting"! I threw my hands up in the air and announced, "Mom, I will never have a gift closet when I grow up!" My dear mom smiled and said, "OK. Just never say never."

I went to my room with my head held high and designed a handmade card for my friend. At the time, a card with oodles of stickers and glitter seemed like a better idea than anything in that "smorgasbord" closet.

It's true that many youngsters tell themselves they will be their own people and not like their parents when they grow up. So of course I had a gift closet in my first apartment when I grew up to be a big girl. It was stocked with the most amazing gifts! I told myself *my* gift closet was completely different from the one with which I grew up. My friends always seemed to give the best gifts, which, in turn, allowed me to have great gifts in my closet. Of course, I did have a few other things in the closet that were less exciting, but there was *always* something for *everyone* in my gift closet.

I was never bothered by turning a year older because I might be able to add another "something wonderful" to my gift closet stash. I loved all birthdays and any other occasion that involved gift-giving, and I especially loved receiving anything monogrammed or with my name on it. There was a time when I thought I should only start accepting new friends with my same initials or name. It would make regifting a whole lot easier! I may have scared a few Jills away with my excitement in discovering we shared a name. If only they would have known what their birthdays or Christmas had in store for them in the form of my gift closet!

So here was Oprah, looking for people to come on her show who were just like me—regifters! My dream of going to *The Oprah*

Winfrey Show finally seemed as if it might happen. I took the next few minutes and typed out the first three stories that popped into my head. They happened to be funny stories, so they were easy to tell. I wrote the episodes as if I were seated beside her on a plane, sharing experiences.

> There was a time when I thought I should only start accepting new friends with my same initials or name. It would make regifting a whole lot easier!

I began with a mishap my twin brother had with regifting a few years prior. Jeff had recently married lovely Allison. Following their wedding reception they hopped on a flight to the beach for their honeymoon. When they returned, their new home was filled with unopened wedding gifts.

After everything was opened, Jeff couldn't remember seeing a gift from me, and he called to jokingly ask where my wedding gift was. I admitted the gift was ordered a little late, only to find it was back-ordered. "It will be there soon, Jeff." I felt awful. Suddenly I revealed, "It's the big tool set on your bridal registry." I had paid for gift wrapping and had it shipped directly to them. I hung up the phone with Jeff, who never mentioned he'd received that same tool set from someone else. When the gift finally arrived, he didn't open the package since he knew what it was. Instead, he shelved my gift in his garage, thinking he would open it shortly and exchange it for something else.

As it happened, my brother forgot about the gift in his garage. Months down the road a college friend was getting married. As

Jeff and Allison were leaving to attend the wedding, they each thought the other had purchased a gift to put in the car. Since Jeff is my mother's son and she taught us well, he knew there would be something around the house that would work for a gift, especially considering they had recently received so many nice presents themselves. He stumbled across my still-wrapped wedding gift. Knowing it was a tool set, he grabbed the gift and never thought twice about it.

A few weeks later Jeff received an email from his friend with a picture of the tool set. There was a card still attached to the wrapping paper: "To Jeff and Allison. I love you both so very much, Jill." The email had two words: "Thanks, Buddy," with a smiley face.

The next story relates an experience that happened to Jeff's twin sister. This would be me. It was almost Christmas, and one of the partners in my law firm gifted me with a beautiful poinsettia and a barrel of Moose Munch popcorn. I thanked him for his thoughtfulness, and we wished each other "Merry Christmas" as he returned to his office.

It was a busy day. I had to prepare for a meeting with a potential new client. The client was in the hospital recovering from an accident, and I was getting ready to hop in my car to meet her for the first time. Wishing I had thought to get a gift to cheer her up, I spotted the gifts on my desk and grabbed them.

As the client and I made small talk, a point of interest surfaced having nothing to do with her accident. I learned she was a friend of the same attorney who had just gifted me the poinsettia and Moose Munch! I spent the rest of the meeting hoping they weren't good enough friends to speak of the gift I had just regifted; however, they were not just friends but very good friends!

My new client called him that evening to tell him how nice it was of me to bring her a gift. She shared with this *very good* friend that Moose Munch popcorn is her favorite, and the poinsettia would perfectly complete her Christmas decorations when she got home. The next morning my *very good* attorney friend came to my office, and we had a good laugh. At least one of us did. I was laughing but on the outside only. Inwardly, I was cringing with embarrassment.

I ended the letter to Oprah with one last story of regifting gone wrong. This tale involved my mother-in-law. I remember vividly how excited she was for me to open the birthday gift she had bought. (My wonderful in-laws are two of the most thoughtful people I have ever known or will ever know.) I recall opening this gift, and although I always appreciated anything she gave me, I knew the perfect spot for this year's present—the gift closet. There it would find many other friends and hopefully a potential new home! The gift was an adorable sewing kit plus some other things, all of which would help me become a better wife and hopefully give me some more of the homemaking skills I never quite seemed to embrace. I know my mother-in-law well. By giving this gift, she was not pointing out my shortcomings in hopes that I'd correct them. She simply thought the kit was cute and that I would love it.

Maybe there's a benefit in freely admitting what I am good at and what I am not good at. For instance, I do not mind acknowledging one of my shortcomings can be my second-rate memory. If I want to remember something, I must *intentionally* remember it. If I wanted to recall my mother-in-law giving me this gift, I would have needed to either commit it to memory or repeat a few times, "My mother-in-law gave me the sewing kit and some other fun things for my birthday." This explains why a little over a year later I regifted the exact same kit back to my mother-in-law on her birthday. The reason: I didn't *intentionally* remember it.

I do remember seeing the sewing kit in my gift closet, and I distinctively remember thinking Terry's mom would be the perfect person for it. I just knew she'd think it was a fun gift to receive. I wrapped the kit and signed a pretty card without a worry in the world. In fact, I was proud of the gift I'd chosen and oh so proud I hadn't waited until the last minute to find it. As this loving person opened my present, I watched her face, and it certainly wasn't the look I was aiming for. I very much wanted to impress and love on my mother-in-law and was hoping this gift would be seen as a thoughtful choice made especially with her in mind.

Surprisingly there was no expression on her face as she thanked me for a great present. My mind was going a million miles a minute. "Did I offend her in some way? Am I missing a hidden meaning in what I gave?" And then it hit me. Slowly but surely—ever so surely.

In my embarrassment I apologized and said, "I just knew it was the perfect gift for you, and now I can clearly see why. You had, after all, picked it out for me, so you must have liked it!" We had a good laugh about the episode later that night. As we were laughing, I made myself a promise: From now on, there would be a label on every gift in the closet with the original giver's name so as to never regift to the giver!

Chapter 4

OPRAH

I EMAILED MY STORIES to Oprah and then gave my attention to legal research for a new case. Two short hours later my secretary buzzed me. "Hi, Jill. Maria from *The Oprah Winfrey Show* is on the line asking to speak to you about your email." For a moment I thought someone from my office was playing a cruel joke. I then realized I hadn't left the office since the email was sent. There was no way anyone could have known I'd just written Oprah.

After taking a deep breath, I did my best to speak calmly, with a casual response. "Hi there. This is Jill."

"Hi, Jill. My name is Maria, and I'm a producer with *The Oprah Winfrey Show*. We are doing a program on all things etiquette later this week. After reading your submission, we were wondering if you would possibly like to be a part of it."

"Um...may I have a little while to think about it?" A millisecond passed. "That sounds like a great idea. I'm in!"

Just like that, the five years of busy signals or "I'm sorry, we are full for the rest of the season" faded away. A new reality was beginning. Maria said the show wanted to fly a producer out to Tulsa to film my gift closet and conduct an interview with me. I tried to mask my excitement and to keep from squealing while responding. In my effort to act calm, I pretty much spoke in a whisper. Maria thought we had a bad connection. "Jill, I'm sorry, but I couldn't hear you. Did you say you are interested and available to film tomorrow?" I cleared my throat. "Absolutely, Maria! Can't wait!"

She went on to tell me the show would be about etiquette, such as regifting and chewing gum in public. We finished the call with the details on when, where, what, and how everything would take place for the filming. After we hung up, I was in a rush to get home and to make sure my gift closet was organized and ready for its unveiling. Then I thought, "There are a few gaps in the closet from having recently gifted to a few friends and family. I've got to fill the shelves by the time the producer flies here tomorrow!"

I headed over to Utica Square shopping center to pick up some additional gifts to enhance the "amazing" closet. As I made purchases, the charges began adding up quickly. I made a mental note to return some of the purchases the day after the interview. The reasoning was sound, I told myself, in that the returned goods would possibly air on *The Oprah Winfrey Show* to millions of viewers. I was really giving the stores free advertising. No harm in that! (If you happen to be a Utica Square business owner, I sincerely apologize for the returns. At the time, I deduced it was a win-win situation: my gift closet would be TV ready, and your inventory would get some visibility. Imagine—free airtime!)

That evening, interspersed with going over and over the story with a wide-eyed husband, I reorganized all the gifts. We stepped back to marvel at the masterpiece. My gift closet had never looked better, and I decided a good night's rest would help me be on my *A game* the next day.

And it all went great. Videoing didn't take up much of the day at all. The producer showed up at our home; the associates set up the equipment; we started shooting right away. The interview was extremely relaxed as I sat down to explain how my regifting closet was carried over from childhood. Sharing the comical stories was a fun part of the shoot. I wanted to keep the interview amusing and lighthearted because I liked laughing more than crying. We wrapped up, and the producer, along with her team, was on her way back to Chicago within hours.

Before they left for the airport, the producer informed me that the video would be shown to other producers working on the same story. Maria would keep me posted on whether they were going to use the clip from Tulsa. There was still no mention of any tickets or even getting to sit in the overflow room during a show. Although I am not shy, I didn't want to be pushy and ask for tickets. I thought, "Just let things happen naturally." I know, I know...after five years of calling and trying to get tickets, now I'm deciding to go natural?

Maria called the very next day, saying the producers loved the gift closet shoot with the interview. "We want to fly you and your husband to Chicago to sit in the front row in the audience, and Oprah will show the video clip. The camera will pan over to you while Oprah thanks you for sharing your story and coming to the show. What do you say?" For sure, it was an easy yes.

What fun this was going to be! Moreover I was finally going to get the closure I longed to have for this hobby. The hours were moving so quickly that it felt dreamlike and much like a whirlwind. Or a combination of the two—a "dreamwind." Maria explained they wanted my husband and me to arrive in Chicago the next day, and the TV taping would start the day after our arrival.

Terry and I arrived in the Windy City midday. (Considering

what was happening, it appeared Chicago was more like the *whirl-wind* city!) We made a quick trip to Nordstrom for a pair of heels, then had dinner, and afterward we settled in our hotel room for the evening. There'd be an early morning pickup, so I wanted to be well-rested for the morrow.

Instead of sleeping, I lay in bed staring wide-eyed at the ceiling for more than half the night. To say I was filled with anticipation would be an understatement. What I was feeling can better be described as a mixture of nervousness and excitement. I was, as my oldest daughter, Ireland, calls it, "nervited"!

During the night, my thoughts wandered back to a childhood memory of a short-lived idea that I would be a newscaster one day. While reflecting on this long-forgotten memory, I must have drifted off to sleep for a little while. I dreamed Oprah and I connected as friends right away. She soon asked me to join her team, which meant appearing weekly as her cohost.

In my dream Oprah said she had hired Dr. Phil and now only needed Dr. Jill to join them. Dr. Jill? Well, I was a newscaster with, of all things, a doctorate degree. To my dismay, when I woke up, I couldn't remember the beginning or the end of the dream. It's a safe bet to assume I accepted her offer. The rest of the night seemed like an eternity, but finally I saw the sun coming up, and the day was finally here!

Terry and I took the elevator down to the colorful hotel café for breakfast. Everything looked delicious, and my dear husband, a gourmet cook, was obviously enjoying it. He kept saying, "Jill, you have to try this. It's prepared so well. You need to eat before we head to the studio." I knew there was no way I could eat in my "nervited" condition. Besides, I did not want to entertain the possibility I might get sick right in the middle of taping.

After Terry had breakfast, a driver came to take us directly to the studio. In the shiny black vehicle I rambled on and on to Terry,

"This dream of getting tickets to the show will have its closure with this trip. Not only are we going to be in the audience, but there will be a video, and Oprah will actually thank us for being there!"

> "Jill, there's been a slight change of plans. You are going to be sitting on the couch with Oprah and we would like for you to share a few of your regifting stories after your video airs."

We arrived at the studio and were greeted by Maria, who was every bit as fun and kind as I had imagined. We were led to a green room, where a makeup artist worked wonders on me, and then I changed into my outfit and new shoes. Subsequently we were swept away and escorted to our seats, and we settled in before the other audience members started arriving. I would have loved to have interviewed them, beginning with, "And how many years did you wait to get tickets?"

As we waited and I practiced breathing, out of the corner of my eye I saw Maria walking toward me, smiling from ear to ear. "Jill, there's been a slight change of plans. You are going to be sitting on the couch with Oprah, and we would like for you to share a few of your regifting stories after your video airs."

It was more than I could have asked for.

More than I even knew was possible.

The couch?

The couch?

The same one that had seated countless movie stars, singers, heroes, generals, senators, philanthropists, foreign dignitaries, scientists, surgeons, Olympians, Kermit the Frog, Miss Piggy, and

US presidents and their First Ladies—the couch Tom Cruise had just crazily jumped up and down on during his recent appearance? (I guess I can't say with absolute certainty it was the *exact* couch, but it was the same color. That was close enough.)

Maria sat me down on *the* couch. I was staring at the space next to me where Oprah would be sitting. Maria smiled and enthusiastically encouraged me with, "Have fun, and good luck!" Then she walked off the stage.

As had happened during other high-stress situations in my life, I suddenly felt a peace wash over me. The makeup artist came to apply more powder and turned the mirror so I could see. "You look great. Do you like it?" I smiled and nodded my head. "Yes! Thank you so much for helping me get ready today."

As she left the set, there was this wonderful calm in my heart. I felt lovely having had my makeup done professionally, felt my outfit was perfect for the occasion, and felt wedding-day beautiful! I sure was ready to get this show on the road!

The audience members were in their seats, and I could see Terry sitting in the front row. He gave me that smile I had seen a hundred times before, the one that said without words, "I'm proud of you. You got this. I love you."

Seated on a couch nearby were two etiquette experts looking as cute as can be. They had big grins on their faces, and as I smiled back, one of them mouthed the words "I love your shoes!" to me. I mouthed back to her, "Thank you." I thought, "This is great! The experts and I are already best friends!" Oprah suddenly appeared and sat down beside me. It literally felt as if we were on a plane getting ready to fly somewhere special. She also pointed toward my feet and said, "Great shoes!" I replied, "Thank you!" While wondering if we were the same shoe size, I heard the sound of the stage lights being switched on. The producers asked for everyone to be silent.

Oprah started the show by speaking into the camera and then to the audience. A few minutes later the video of my gifting closet was playing on a big screen. There were lots of laughs from the audience, and when the video ended, Oprah turned to me and asked me what I thought now that I had been exposed to the world.

I really did feel a bit exposed with the realization the entire nation (and beyond) would be viewing my special closet. I was hoping to get some laughs with an amusing reply, but Oprah had turned to my two best friends sitting just one couch over, the etiquette experts from Canada, to hear what they had to say.

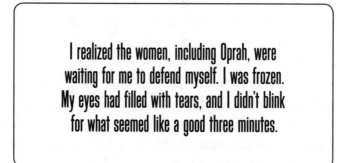

I realized the women, including Oprah, were waiting for me to defend myself. I was frozen. My eyes had filled with tears, and I didn't blink for what seemed like a good three minutes.

I want to pause here to share that the night before we left for Chicago, I googled "etiquette and regifting." What did the etiquette world think of regifting, and how should I respond to questioning? I read that what I did was totally acceptable if I didn't lie. (Obviously I wasn't lying since I was telling the world about this practical idea on national television.) I was positive these experts would enjoy seeing the unique and carefully selected gifts as well as noticing the fine organization.

I was completely unprepared for the experts' response. They

criticized my idea and my reasoning throughout the program. The two etiquette experts from Canada thought my regifting was rude, tacky, and wrong. They were in agreement that what I did was completely unacceptable, cheesy, and fraudulent.

Suddenly the entire world was moving in slow motion. I saw the two women's mouths moving, but I couldn't hear anything above the buzzing in my head. I trusted that at any moment they'd burst into laughter, saying, "Just kidding! We love you and can't wait to see you more often on *Oprah*." That never happened. Instead, they continued to say that everything—yes, *everything* in the closet— needed to be donated to charity.

Then there was a pause, and Oprah was looking at me as if she was waiting for my response. I realized the women, including Oprah, were waiting for me to defend myself. I was frozen. My eyes had filled with tears, and I didn't blink for what seemed like a good three minutes. Only seconds had gone by, though. Not only was I speechless, but I was bug-eyed staring into the audience, too afraid to blink for fear the tears would pour down my face. How could I defend myself? I was not prepared to do such a thing but only to tell funny stories and make everyone laugh. (I had chosen *not* to be a defense attorney for good reason!)

I've heard some people, in order to deal with extreme nerves when facing a crowd, choose to imagine that the audience forgot to get dressed for the occasion. This helps lighten the anxiety. I experienced tunnel vision instead and immediately zoned in on the experts' eyes, imagining they both had unibrows. With that visualization the only response I could think of was, "Well, we must do things a little differently in America than what is the norm for you in Canada. For instance, we pluck between the eyebrows." I did not want to defend myself and decided against saying anything that might hurt their feelings. I went for humor. I am sure they both had perfectly shaped and plucked eyebrows.

The show finally ended, and I headed straight for Maria, standing left of stage. "Maria, that didn't quite turn out like I had imagined. If possible, could you please not air my segment?"

"Jill, it really wasn't as bad as you think."

"Well, from my viewpoint, it felt like I was on a sinking ship, so is there anything I can do to keep you from airing my part?"

My negotiations led nowhere, and I left the studio with a sick feeling in the pit of my stomach—the feeling you get when you have no desire to socialize, smile, or ever eat again.

Chapter 5

GINO'S PIZZERIA

B<small>UT...</small>I <small>DID EAT</small> again. After the show Terry and I went to Chicago's iconic Gino's pizzeria. Yes, I was an emotional mess, horribly embarrassed by the show, but I was also starving since I hadn't eaten. How could I deny my consoling husband's offer to feed me Gino's pizza?

Were there tears? They began to pour out at the studio and continued at the restaurant. The pizza was mixed with reliving the experience and with descriptions of my hurting ego from the entire experience. I knew the pain was inconsequential compared with multitudes who were dealing with larger-than-life issues: death, divorce, affliction, job loss, and the struggle to provide for one's family. But in a moment I had gone from the highest of highs to the lowest of lows—absolute and complete humiliation. Life can turn on a dime. And mine had, but it bears repeating: In the grand scheme of things my pain was minimal compared with what others suffered. Yet I know that pain is pain—no matter the source.

I had believed a dream would be fulfilled, but the cost brought me mortification on national television. My head spun with "I should have stayed with my original plan to be a member of the audience. Why did I take it a step further? Why, oh why, did I volunteer to be on the show?" As we sat at the table, I saw sympathy in Terry's eyes and said to him, "I do not know the significance of what happened, but I *do* know that one day this pain will serve a purpose in some capacity of my life." This assurance was the only sense of clarity I had that day. For some reason God allowed me to have this one lucid moment. *He didn't want me to forget it either.* I like to call this my "Gino's pizza moment."

As soon as we returned home, I emptied the gift closet. There was no need for this closet since I'd made up my mind my regifting days were over. I put everything in trash bags (other than the returns), and Terry donated them to charity. As I stared at the empty closet, my only thought was, "I will never fill this closet again." I just wanted to forget anything that could awaken the emotions from that day. Desiring to protect myself from these kinds of feelings was instrumental in the decision to leave the closet empty. This way I would never need to open that door.

> "I do not know the significance of what happened, but I *do* know that one day this pain will serve a purpose in some capacity of my life."

The case was closed; however, it took three weeks after the Chicago trip to get through even a day without my stomach turning.

The slightest remembrance of what had happened was a powerful trigger. I even convinced myself the show might never air. No one would ever see it, aside from the audience of three hundred who witnessed my humiliation.

Then my phone rang.

It was Maria calling me.

"Jill, guess what? Call all your friends because the show is going to air!"

I responded, "Maria, guess what? I won't have any friends if the show airs." She laughed and said the show was great, wonderfully entertaining, and everyone would love it. Just as Maria reported, the show aired. It was even more upsetting to watch on TV than what I recalled from sitting on the couch. I remember going out to dinner that evening with Terry. A sweet girl came up to me and eagerly asked, "You look so familiar. How do I know you?"

I told her: "I think it may be because I look like Mary Lou Retton, the Olympic gymnast. A few others have mentioned that to me. It's the short hair. Or there's Suze Orman, the financial coach—I get mistaken for her occasionally." But I knew full well she had just seen *The Oprah Winfrey Show*!

Around six months later I received another call from Maria. "Jill! Your episode was one of our highest-rated shows this year, and it's going to air a second time. Call all your friends again!" And that's exactly what I did. I called all my friends in tears, looking to be consoled or perhaps cheered up in some way.

Within one year my episode aired three times, with approximately twenty million viewers each time. This meant many millions of people thought of me as tacky and rude. My heart was having trouble bearing that thought. To move forward and put the memory of a "good thing gone bad" behind me, I decided to swear off all new hobbies and only concentrate on my family. I also accepted an offer to be an adjunct law professor. I wanted to suppress the fact that there was a perfectly good closet going to waste. Useless.

That is, until five years later...I decided it was time to open the closet again. Yet this time I would fill the closet with my *own* creations—my own type of gifting closet of sorts. (Oh well, this meant my family would still have no linen closet filled with sheets and towels like the rest of our friends had.) It was in that moment, when the idea came to create my own gifts, that I finally realized the pain carried from the *Oprah* show was going to serve a purpose.

> **Within one year my episode aired three times, with approximately twenty million viewers each time. This meant many millions of people think of me as tacky and rude.**

I had the hope that my moment of clarity at Gino's pizzeria years ago was finally beginning to unfold and the disappointment and ache I felt that day would have been worth it, as there was a greater plan I had no idea even existed.

Little did I know...

PART II
FOR THE LOVE OF QUOTES

Inspirational quotes are important because they activate an emotional pulse point in our hearts and minds when we are in a distressing situation. The right quote can help us to see light at the end of the tunnel, and give us that extra burst of hope and courage to persevere.[1]
—MICHEL F. BOLLE

Chapter 6

THE BEST TIME FOR A NEW BEGINNING IS RIGHT NOW

As each day passed after what I still consider my most embarrassing and humbling moment, the rawness of it all was also passing...little by little. Eventually I forgave "the experts." Operating out of fear, I decided not to ever place myself in a vulnerable position again. Previously I mentioned there would *be no more hobbies*. But then, as part of the forgiveness process, I cautiously allowed myself to consider whether I might once again find a creative outlet. The yearning was there to do something that would satisfy the imaginative bent within me. I thought about this often.

One night after everyone in my home was sound asleep, at around 2 a.m., I was watching a little bit of reality television. On-screen was a woman demonstrating how she makes her own jewelry and cuffs. It resonated with me because I had a love for all things cuffs/bracelets.

It all started with American Airlines. When I worked for that company, I was given a certain number of passes to take trips during the year. Oddly enough, there was always a cuff with me on the return trip. It was a keepsake from the foreign city I visited. By the time I parted with American Airlines, I had an entire drawer filled with amazing cuffs. Some people collect magnets from their travels, and others collect coffee mugs from theirs—I collected beautiful cuffs. I would open my drawer of roughly a dozen cuffs, and each one of them could tell a story about the experience I had in that particular location.

My mind began racing: "Was that woman on TV really making them? Or was that just a front for the sake of the show? Is this something she taught herself and is now pursuing beyond just a hobby? If she can do this, I can do this!" A light bulb had gone on, and I jumped out of bed to start researching.

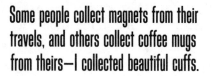

Some people collect magnets from their travels, and others collect coffee mugs from theirs—I collected beautiful cuffs.

I searched Google and YouTube for hours throughout the night, soaking up every idea on the best way to make cuffs. I could not get enough information. But for once it didn't feel like work! I was so driven to teach myself this new skill that I wanted to do nothing but lock myself in a room with a computer and as many supplies as I needed to get started.

For the next several months I worked on creating cuffs without telling anyone. I took $250 to a leather store to purchase materials and sat with the employees, who were just as eager to teach me as I was to learn. The manager of the store, Judy, became such an amazing resource for me that every time I enter her store to this day, I am filled with so much gratitude for her time and confidence that I could learn and create anything I wanted to without barriers. She was patient beyond belief, and I have never met a store manager who truly wanted to see someone succeed the way Judy did.

For the next four months I got very little sleep, spending most nights in our guest bedroom working on cuffs. I would put my daughters to bed and work while everyone slept. Eventually I'd make myself go to bed and sleep for a few hours before the new day began. Through the research and lots of trial and error, in due course I figured out what worked and what didn't.

Eventually I started making a few personalized leather cuffs as gifts for family and friends. There was no intention of starting another regifting closet and absolutely no intention of starting a business. I wanted to raise our daughters, continue to learn how to cook (OK, that's a stretch), play tennis, and have this cuff-making as my creative outlet.

However, working with not enough sleep was taking its toll. One morning I woke the girls up for school a few minutes early. I wanted to get their opinion on a cuff I had made while they were asleep. Their response was less than excited: "Mom, it's Saturday. Let us go back to bed." Come to find out, my lack of sleep was making me quite forgetful.

Another day the girls came to the guest bedroom, where I was working, because they were hungry. I said, "You guys, I just fed you on Monday. How often do you really need to eat?" They looked at me sideways with smiles and said, "Mom, it's Thursday." (To comfort those who might be concerned, please know I had full faith that Terry had stepped up to the plate and made certain the girls were well fed.)

The first cuff I ever gave away was to my sweet friend Katie, who had just had her first little girl. I had engraved her daughter's name on it and given it to her as a gift. Katie wore the cuff for a week or so and called me, saying, "You have to start selling these." I responded with, "No way! It's just for fun!" Then she announced, "I already have about twenty-two people who want their own custom cuff. What's the price?" I blurted out, "Thirty-eight dollars," and those twenty-two people were the first buyers of my rustic-looking leather cuffs.

One afternoon after I started selling cuffs, my daughters were helping by sorting cuffs to fill orders, and Terry asked, "If this is going to be a business, shouldn't there be a name?" We brainstormed for a while, and I came up with Cuff Love. But for some reason, after I had a few business cards made with that name, it just didn't feel like the right puzzle piece. It wasn't long after that I came up with Rustic Cuff, as most every single cuff I was creating had that rustic look. Little did I know that *rustic* was not the only style of cuff I was going to fall in love with.

> I figured if I was going to be up creating cuffs, it would be more fun if my TV friends who kept me company were wearing them as well!

Then I thought, "If I'm going to have a business with a name, how should I advertise?" Ugh, I couldn't stand the idea of pushing my cuffs on someone. As I wrote in my "*never* list," I never wanted to have employees, so it goes without saying I never wanted a business. I really had been quite happy just making cuffs for friends or family members who wanted them. Since there had been no business model to start with, there was no advertising plan either.

I continued teaching law and found myself increasingly filling orders for cuffs from all around Tulsa, not just for people I knew. I loved making the bracelets and did so during the day, and once the girls went to bed, I'd fashion new designs while watching TV. The shows were recorded on my DVR from daytime TV. One night while watching a panel talk show, I thought it would be neat if someone had a Rustic Cuff bracelet on her wrist...someone outside of Tulsa and outside of my group of friends. The hosts of these TV shows began to feel like friends to me. They even felt like my cheerleaders on some level since they were with me in the middle of the night as the cuffs were being created. I had an idea.

On a big whiteboard I had bought for the guest bedrooms, I wrote all of the names of my night-owl friends who had been keeping me company for months. I had taken notice of their individual on-air jewelry styles, and each box had five to seven cuffs that I felt my "cheerleaders" would like. The packaging I'd designed was sleek and professional-looking, so there'd be no way of knowing that what they received was handmade on my guest bedroom floor. I also did extra research on their children's names, anniversary dates, and other significant moments to put on some of the cuffs. I figured if I was going to be up creating cuffs, it would be more fun if my TV friends who kept me company were wearing them as well!

When each box was complete, I went straight to UPS to ship them overnight. Every night I turned on the recording from earlier in the day to watch a show that featured a celebrity I had sent cuffs to. I hoped I would see someone wearing one of my creations.

Then one day I was watching Kathie Lee Gifford and Barry Manilow talking away on her show. He'd just performed a song, and before they cut to commercial, Kathie Lee reached out to touch his shoulder. I couldn't believe what I spotted. Kathie Lee was wearing a cuff from the box I had just shipped to her! (Not to mention it was on the arm that had just touched Barry Manilow, one of my favorite singers in the whole wide world!) I hit the rewind button probably a million times—I watched the clip over and over to make sure I wasn't dreaming.

It was surreal when I started seeing other well-known people wearing cuffs from the boxes I had shipped. One afternoon I was at the airport, and I was looking through a magazine that had done an interview with Miranda Lambert. Lo and behold, she was wearing one of the cuffs I had just sent her a few weeks before the issue came out. It was quite surreal to realize I could make a cuff on Tuesday, overnight it on Wednesday, and turn on morning TV Friday and see the very same cuff I had just sent.

> It's not really about the cuffs at all but about the people. It's about the stories, joys, and heartaches we all share. And it includes learning how to be there for one another during those times.

I had no business plan, no advertising plan. No plan felt right to me, but I couldn't think of better advertising than having people in all walks of life wearing cuffs I had created. The idea worked, and suddenly I was overcome with orders and questions about Rustic Cuff from around the country. Then came the realization I could not keep up with the emails and voice mails. The thought arose to temporarily hire someone to help catch up so each person could be taken care of.

Around that time I was introduced to a girl who had a charming personality whom I just loved. There I was, hiring Meagen, my first employee. Wanting to be transparent with her from the beginning,

I told her I wasn't sure how I was going to be able to pay her. But as of today she has yet to go without a paycheck. (Whew!) Shortly the two of us realized we needed a couple more people to help us. That need for a few more turned to twenty, and as of this writing I employ about 220 remarkable people.

In the summer of 2012, eleven days after hiring Meagen, I was fortunate to cross paths with Tory Johnson. Tory hosts ABC's *Good Morning America*'s popular weekly "Deals & Steals" and curates all the products for *The View*'s "View Your Deal." Not only is she one of the most savvy businesswomen I know, but she also quickly became a friend and mentor. Tory asked me that summer if I would be willing to have Rustic Cuff on GMA as one of the highlighted products for an upcoming week. I'd sure like to say I was the one who took a chance by answering yes, but it was Tory who took a chance on me.

We sold two thousand cuffs when the segment aired. My thoughts remain a bit foggy as to how Meagen and I, as well as fifteen of my friends whom I persuaded to join us, made it through the next couple of weeks. It was amazing that we were able to produce and ship so many unexpected orders quickly following the program. In looking back, the experience cemented our thoughts that we were right where we were supposed to be. Tory took a big chance on me that day, and she serves as a constant reminder that sometimes this is all it takes to give someone hope that anything is possible.

If I had been shown the road map ahead of me, I would have run in the opposite direction. In hindsight, however, I see that my drive to have a new hobby each year and to be disciplined was preparation for what lay ahead. These yearly goals were training and prepping me for the big challenge and joy that is today called Rustic Cuff.

I'm so glad I didn't run away. Instead, daily I go to the place we call our office, which feels more like summer camp. We never want to leave! And instead of spending Sundays dreading the upcoming week, I can't wait for the week to begin. I love our customers and the people I work with so much that sometimes it's hard for me to fall asleep, anticipating what is to come. It's like thinking about Santa coming down the chimney—on repeat.

At times people have driven by one of our showrooms, only to see a line of people waiting to get in. I'll take a guess they say to themselves, "I would never stand in a line that long for a bracelet." I actually might have thought the same thing. But if you ever did decide to stand in that line, you'd most likely appreciate that it's not really about the cuffs at all but about the people. It's about the stories, joys, and heartaches we all share. And it includes learning how to be there for one another during those times.

Eventually I started creating engraved cuffs with quotes that are meaningful. In a time of need I wanted someone to be able to look down at her wrist and instantly see a phrase, a quote, that is encouraging. Or if that person came across someone else who was struggling, I wanted the bracelet's owner to have a real peace about giving the quote cuff away because she just *knew* it would make a difference.

The following chapters include some of my favorite quotes relating to stories that are etched in my heart. Some chapters relate directly to Rustic Cuff; others simply were birthed from mean-ingful quotes seen on a cuff. May these stories stir your soul in some way and cause you to be inspired.

Chapter 7

ONE DAY AT A TIME

D O YOU REMEMBER the show *The Newlywed Game*? Each couple would try to match each other's answers to random questions. Well, if you ask my husband, Terry, "What is one thing Jill does that you think needs improvement?" his answer would most certainly be, "Make analogies."

Terry thinks I overuse analogies, and yes, I admit it. Guilty as charged. But I cannot find a better story to describe how I felt five years ago when the journey of Rustic Cuff began. (Terry, this is where you might want to skip ahead a few chapters.)

Many, many years ago there was this man named Noah. He was minding his own business, taking care of his family, and playing a little tennis here and there. (No, wait. That tennis part was me. I can see why Terry has some concerns. Let's continue.) Noah was enjoying life with family and friends when God instructed him to build the most massive boat anyone had ever seen or even imagined. How could Noah not be worried? How could he, a mere man, take on such a colossal project? I can picture the thoughts going through his mind: "What if I get seasick? What if I am allergic to some of the animals?" (Being painfully aware of my own motion sickness, I would have wanted to ask, "How many days will I be on the boat? I want to make sure I have enough Dramamine.") But none of that mattered to Noah because he knew God had a plan and could be trusted with the whole enterprise.

So Noah obeyed God, carrying out every instruction without worry, working with one plank at a time. His faith would carry him through daily. Noah most likely had to remind himself quite often that he was not the captain of the ark, nor was the ark designed to be steered or even sailed. The ship would drift as God willed.

Here is where I draw an analogy. A few years after cleaning out my entire gift closet and swearing off regifting for life, I was in bed watching TV, and it was as if I were handed three things: a hammer, a bag of nails, and two planks. A single instruction was given: "Hammer the two planks together, and each day you will get one additional plank." Of course I had some great arguments:

1. I'm not a builder.

2. I don't know how to read a blueprint.

3. I'm allergic to splinters.

> I had one and only one responsibility: not to worry about my tomorrows. It was almost like an eleventh commandment. What freedom to know that tomorrow is not my worry.

But none of that mattered. This was an "ark" I would not have created on my own, nor would I have even come close to calling it an ark at this point. It seemed more like a canoe or a small sail-boat. Additionally no one had dropped off a schematic or any kind of draft at my home.

Yet each day, without fail, I was handed another "plank"—each one varying in length and weight. Some days it was obvious as to where to insert a plank. Other days I would need to sit still while waiting to know where to put it.

The beauty of knowing this—and I mean *really* knowing this—was that I did not need to worry about tomorrow's plank. I wasn't concerned with my ability to lift it, where it should be placed, or what its purpose was. The thing required was for me to focus on the direction for that day. I didn't ponder whether it all made sense or worry about criticism regarding the look of my planks. Like Noah, I didn't have a plan of my own.

I had one and only one responsibility: not to worry about my tomorrows. It was almost like an eleventh commandment. What freedom to know that tomorrow is not my worry. Fretting over what may come can't change the future any more than wishing or regretting can change the past. What's more, living in yesterday or tomorrow robs us of the joy of today. It steals our peace.

One of the most requested cuffs, one that is both gifted to others and kept, is the quote cuff engraved with "One day at a time."

That saying can mean different things to different people. Just as Noah never imagined building the ark, I couldn't imagine starting a company from scratch or even writing a book, for that matter. Both of us realized the necessity of accepting instructions without seeing the full purpose behind the initial plan.

We don't need to know what tomorrow holds; we simply need

to know who holds tomorrow. The next time you find yourself living in the past or beyond today, remember, you only need to live *one day at a time*—or, if you are a fan of analogies, *one "plank" at a time*.

> Fretting over what may come can't change the future any more than wishing or regretting can change the past. What's more, living in yesterday or tomorrow robs us of the joy of today.

Chapter 8

EXPECT NOTHING; APPRECIATE EVERYTHING

I T's ONE THING to write a book about my observations and experiences with irrational generosity and kindness. It's an entirely different ball game to be on the *receiving* end of unexpected, irrational kindness. When one is on the receiving end, a lasting imprint is left on the soul. Through experience I've learned the most amazing moments and unexpected acts of kindness start happening in my life when I fully embrace "Expect nothing; appreciate everything."

A couple of years ago I had the occasion to donate some money to an auction for the Chris Evert Foundation. (Tennis was her game and mine too for years.) The auction ended with my getting the opportunity to spend an hour having tea in London with the Duchess of York, Sarah Ferguson. Many years ago I read of the friendship between princesses Diana and Sarah, both daughters-in-law of the Queen of England. Their stories captured the attention of millions, and I was no exception. I was elated to have a royal experience waiting for me on the horizon.

Two years flew by as we tried to coordinate schedules. (I like using those words because it almost gives me duchess status if I phrase it that way!) But we finally did orchestrate a date for tea, and I counted down the days for the flight across the ocean.

It's a little embarrassing to admit, but I had never had a cup of tea in my life. Unless you count the time I had "tea" with my daughters when they were two and five years old—in Hello Kitty cups with watered-down apple juice. Needless to say, I definitely had room for tea-sipping improvement.

My assistants Meagen and Jordan were flying to London with me. The three of us were unfamiliar with British manners, so it made perfect sense to hire an etiquette expert. At least we'd have some basic knowledge under our extended pinkie fingers to keep from making fools of ourselves while downing...English tea.

> It's generally at this moment that the magic happens with me—the moment when I realize all my expectations need to go.

The etiquette expert, Rachel Wagner, was lovely as well as non-judgmental, especially when we expressed wide-eyed surprise each time she shared a new tip. We had basically done everything backward our whole lives—at least when it came to drinking tea with any royals. For instance, I have been folding a napkin in my lap incorrectly all my years. Amazingly the three of us also learned we could use a knife and fork in sign language to communicate with a waiter, though this didn't permit one to wave silverware in the air to get the server's attention. Moreover when we finished a meal, we were to place the knife and fork in a specific position on the plate as a signal to the waiter.

The etiquette tutor ended our lesson with, in my opinion, the best part. She taught us the correct way to curtsy and say, "Your grace." I knew the etiquette tips would serve us well and leave the duchess with a good impression of three Midwestern girls. How *splendid* (a word Brits would use) to have all these manners to draw from on our journey. On March 30, 2017, we would be delicately sipping tea with an elegant duchess in the usually foggy London town.

When March 30, 2017, finally arrived, surprisingly it was a bright, sunny day in London, and I couldn't wait to test my new skills at a royal tea. As we waited in a private room at the Mark's Club in the posh neighborhood of Mayfair, I kept asking the girls, "Are you as nervous as I am to meet the Duchess of York?" They agreed they were equally nervous. I tried to think of something that would help rid us of anxiety so we could be fully in the moment and enjoy it. An idea came right before the duchess was to arrive. My last words to Meagen and Jordan were: "Girls, let's just be ourselves and have zero expectations. I'm so grateful for this fun opportunity. Let's pretend we're meeting an old friend to have an enjoyable conversation. Nothing else." It's generally at this moment that the magic happens with me—the moment when I realize all my expectations need to go.

A few minutes later the duchess walked in with a bright smile on her face, along with a genuine eagerness to meet with us. She was just as spunky and charming as I had imagined...and then some! Sarah Ferguson is very relatable and showed true interest in learning about us and our lives in Oklahoma. I felt a connection to her. She reminded me of someone I might have grown up with yet hadn't seen in years. You know how that goes—you pick up right where you left off the last time together. Delightful! And she was.

At this point everything we learned in the etiquette lesson went right out the window. The sign language with the knife and fork, along with the proper way to "cream and sugar" a cup of tea, quickly fled my mind. I even stopped worrying whether a napkin should be forward, backward, inside out, or upside down. "Fergie" seemed just like us and made us feel comfortable in her presence.

After the initial introduction we ladies immediately started sharing stories of our lives. It was clear Sarah operates from a place of transparency. I had heard of the duchess's wonderful openhandedness and her tender heart toward children. It was even more touching to hear her speak of her passions in person. She's generous because she feels it deep within her soul—not out of obligation, nor out of duty to her position, or even for public recognition. It was plain she gets tremendous joy following up on plans that change people's lives for the good.

Unexpectedly her face lit up, and it was obvious she had come up with some sort of idea. Because of her giving heart, Meagen, Jordan, and I found ourselves on the receiving end of her kindness. (This was a morning when the three of us had chosen to have zero expectations!) Looking at us, she asked, "What are you doing tonight?" I replied, "We haven't made plans yet." (We proper ladies hadn't yet decided which new place to try for fish and chips that evening.)

She asked us in her spunky, yet very British, accent, "Would you like to be my guests at a benefit concert at the Royal Albert Hall? Princess Beatrice will join us in the Royal Box." My thoughts: "I'm sorry! What? Did you just ask us, after only minutes with you, if we wanted to be your personal guests at a concert? And sit in the Royal Box?"

Of course we wanted to join her! I think our smiles were as wide as hers when she picked up the phone to call her daughter, Princess Beatrice. They worked out the details to make everything happen in short notice. She then called her driver and asked him to take us on a tour of London in her car. "Our very own duchess" also requested that he be our chauffeur for the evening event.

After about two hours (an hour longer than had been scheduled or expected) on the couch having tea and cookies, exchanging stories, chatting as if our conversation were all that mattered, tea time was over. She turned around to reach behind her chair and handed the three of us large bags of special gifts. This new friend wanted us to have gifts to remember our time in London. Her kindness kept coming when she even blessed us with presents for each one of our children.

> Someone else's irrational generosity, combined with our zero expectations, created something magical.

It would be a vast understatement to say the rest of the day and evening were surreal. Sitting in the Royal Box with new friends that included the duchess, a princess, and an Academy Award winner, Ben Kingsley, was an experience that could not be bought. Talking with Kingsley, who won best actor for *Gandhi*, was quite enriching. *Schindler's List* was a film of his I shall never forget.

I will always treasure the kindness we received that day. As I said earlier, being on the receiving end of another's irrational generosity leaves its mark on you. You may ask me, "What is your most vivid memory of your time in London?" Without hesitation I'd answer, "Watching my new friend Sarah light up with joy when she gifted a once-in-a-lifetime experience to three American girls."

I may never fully comprehend how a tea date with the duchess turned into a nine-hour experience we could only dream about.

What I do know is that someone else's irrational generosity, combined with our zero expectations, created something magical.

Now let me share with you another story, a rather difficult one, that highlights the concept of "Expect nothing; appreciate everything."

I was sixteen years old and had been dating someone special for about a year. My eighteenth birthday was approaching. Greg was enthusiastic about his gift and talked about what he had for me—constantly. Because of his over-the-top excitement my imagination was over the top. I thought, "This is it. Greg is giving me an engagement ring!" In reality it was a bit soon for that, but maybe it'd be a promise ring or a necklace. I imagined wearing one of these every day. Knowing he picked it out just for me would have me beaming! Or…maybe it would be his football letter jacket. My emotions were overflowing with hope.

My birthday finally arrived, and we had plans to celebrate that evening. Greg walked into my home with a gorgeously wrapped gift. He handed it to me with the biggest smile. "Happy birthday! I hope you love this." My excitement grew! I tore through the beautiful ribbons and shiny paper, only to find something that had never entered my mind. It was a wicker basket filled with six miniature people made out of—panty hose! Inside the basket was a little note that read "The Reamer Family." None of us were left out. There was Dad with his black-framed eyeglasses, Mom, and my three brothers. And of course the birthday girl!

I could barely believe what I was seeing. While I fought back tears and hid my expression of disbelief, Greg informed me a friend had made "The Reamer Family" specifically for me. He went on and on, raving about the amount of talent it took to make such a masterpiece. And how about the time expended? He went on to point out each small detail of the panty-hose family.

At this point those details were completely lost on me. There was no way I understood how he could be that excited about this gift, which for weeks had filled me with huge anticipation. Did he really see a panty-hose family and say to himself, "Yes! This is the perfect gift for Jill's seventeenth birthday!" I knew my boyfriend had more plans for the night, so I tried my best to put the panty-hose family behind me.

> With misplaced expectations comes the inability to live in the moment. High expectations steal whatever might come and often bring disappointment and hurt feelings.

During the evening I did all I could to put on a happy face each time Greg brought up the panty-hose family. Hiding my disappointment took a lot of grit. It helped to put the gift in the back of my mind since he had chosen my favorite restaurant for dinner. At least it worked for a little while.

Later, when Greg walked me to my door, he could barely contain his joy when he said, "I hope this has been one of your best birthdays. I am so glad you loved your gift." Once he left, I slowly walked to my bedroom, thinking about the promise ring or necklace I wasn't wearing.

As I was trying to fall asleep, my mind-set started to change. "Hey, I really did have a great birthday with Greg. He was so caring, endearing, and lighthearted. How could I be so disappointed while he was so excited about the panty-hose family? Was it possible I set him up for failure with my high hopes and expectations?"

I came to the realization I had predicted my own outcome. With my prediction I stifled my chance of seeing the spontaneity and creativity of Greg's unique gift. Because of those lofty expectations anything else would leave me feeling disappointed. The bar had been set too high. He could only fail.

With misplaced expectations comes the inability to live in the moment. High expectations steal whatever might come and often bring disappointment and hurt feelings. Let's remind ourselves to look at every interaction as a clean slate and to be fully present.

When I give to someone, I don't want to focus on what the recipient might say or do since it robs me of delighting in the freedom of *just* giving, just helping. When I hold open a door, give a present, sacrifice for another, offer emotional or monetary help—I want to do it with no thought of "payback."

We may never receive the thank-you note we expected or the smile back from the stranger. Let go of it all. Once we grow to "expect nothing and appreciate everything," we get to taste the true magic of giving freely.

Chapter 9

BE FEARLESS IN THE PURSUIT OF WHAT SETS YOUR SOUL ON FIRE

WHEN I TURNED forty years old, I decided I wanted to do something outside my comfort zone. It should be not only something that would be memorable but something that would have an impact on the next forty years. I wanted to attempt a feat I was afraid of and land on the other side of it, not wanting to go around it but run right to it and through it.

Since driving down the highway with a wasp in the car didn't seem like a safe option, I decided to go to my next fear: climbing up a pole—a very small telephone pole, thirty feet high. And then stand straight up, waiting for what I was sure would feel like an eternity and for a partner to come stand next to me, and we'd then jump off together.

I did it! And I have climbed the same thirty-foot pole in Arizona approximately ten more times since that initial jump. Even though I have done the feat quite a few times, my hands still shake, my knees still get weak, and my stomach still has major butterflies—*every single time*. The difference is I *know* that I *know* I can do it.

One of my favorite sayings about the reality of fear is this: "Fear makes the wolf bigger than he is." When you live in fear, everything is larger than life. Every thirty-foot pole seems like a skyscraper. Every fish seems like a shark. Every cloud seems like a major thunderstorm. I choose to look fear straight in the face and say, "You will not paralyze my heart or my mind." Courage teaches our fears a lesson. Trust me.

I learned that every time I practice courage, I gain confidence. Every time we look fear straight in the face and move forward in spite of it, we build a memory in our minds and in our hearts. Courage is a muscle that strengthens every time we use it, and when we add a new memory of courage, here is what that memory tells us: "You have been here before. You lived through this. And you can do this again."

How would it feel if you were to begin your own chapter of courage today and give yourself something to reference tomorrow? You may be facing different circumstances, but the story is the same. God is bigger than any shark, skyscraper, or storm. And hopefully with courage you will keep walking toward it, not running away from it. The beauty of it all is we don't even have to fight our own battles—someone else is. And in that we can relax.

In January of 2017 I posted this question on Facebook to a group of about forty thousand people: "What would you attempt if you knew you could not fail?" (That question is now on one of our quote cuffs.) I asked the readers to write me a note describing what they'd attempt if failure was not a concern. Thinking to receive only a large handful of notes from people expressing their dreams, I was completely overwhelmed with the response of over one thousand letters, some of them up to ten pages long.

> Courage is a muscle that strengthens
> every time we use it.

Many letters spoke of having trouble being fearless in following passions, in following up on possibly long-held dreams. People poured out their hearts expressing what they needed courage for, but because they were afraid of failing, the longings went unfulfilled. Some shared they had been told their dream was an impossible one. And some wrote that circumstances dictated what they could do, so they ended up not reaching for their dreams.

I am writing this chapter while continuing to read responses. There is quite a stack! With each letter I feel as if I am reading a book. The realization: We indeed are all the same. For sure there are differences, but on the most basic level the fear of failure plays a part in all our lives. Imagine what we could do if that fear weren't around to torment us. As I continue to read and make the effort to respond to each letter, I see how some people aren't even able to put one foot in front of the other. Fear may paralyze and stop people in their tracks, which results in the failure they have been fearing all along. In each letter I see a small part of myself. As I respond to a letter, it's as if I am responding to myself, encouraging my heart with the same advice I pen to someone far away.

Here's something that may make a difference: share your dreams with one or more trustworthy people. Share with friends who are comfortable to be with. Allow your imagination to work for you by picturing your desires. See your dreams with fear out of the way.

There is a commonality among all the letters. Reading and responding to them reaffirms two things I can identify with:

- "I have a passion to accomplish _____. I really want to do it!"

- "I can't seem to pick my feet up to take the first step because I am afraid I will fail."

Let me give a couple of practical suggestions: Try writing down three attainable goals for the year. Then write down three goals that are so big you think they are probably unattainable. Write down something that makes you want to leap out of bed in the morning and something that keeps you awake at night with excitement.

> ## See your dreams with fear out of the way.

It could range from something small, such as taking art lessons, all the way to starting the process of adopting a child. No goal is too small or too big if it's something burning in your soul. So many things seem impossible until you get on the other side, and then you realize that they were simply opportunities disguised as impossibilities.

Writing down these goals and talking about them may help materialize them—and how wonderful if it helps you release the fear of failure. Each month revisit the goals you wrote down to see how far you've come and what more you can do to achieve them. Just one small step can be the key to keeping you moving forward, free of irrational fear.

You can be an amazing mom, an outstanding wife, or a dedicated employee. You can be all of these things and yet still have God-given dreams. He made you and gave you your talents and desires for a reason. Start with one goal, one dream, one thing that brings you joy, and watch yourself come alive again.

It always seems impossible until it's done.[1]

—Nelson Mandela

You are never too old to set another goal or to dream a new dream.[2]

—C. S. Lewis

Chapter 10

KINDNESS IS ITS OWN LANGUAGE— STUDY IT UNTIL YOU ARE FLUENT

I N THE EARLY days of Rustic Cuff, before we had multiple showrooms, shopping was an online experience only. We did have office space where the cuffs were made and where we handled customer service calls and emails. There was also a room where some of the cuffs were displayed. Nothing was ever advertised, and there had been no announcement that there was a place to come and shop. However, as word spread about Rustic Cuff, people began coming to our place of business. Week after week more and more people came to see what Rustic Cuff was all about.

The office's allotted space for working was perfect in size, but it was less than ideal for retail. The display area quickly became crowded as more and more people started showing up. Not only was it crowded inside the showroom, but there were lines of customers wrapped around the building, waiting to come through one green wooden door. Sometimes these lines were hours long before a customer could even step into the office. The waiting crowd would stand or sit outside in a line, some having brought lawn chairs and coolers. Once they made it through the door, it wasn't always easy to move around. The few employees in the display room were aware of the fire code and tried to be compliant. An employee would be at the door to curb the number of people coming into the new cuff wonderland.

I particularly remember one busy Saturday, with the usual line of customers waiting about three to four hours to make it through the door. That day we had six checkout lines inside to facilitate shoppers more quickly, and the desire was to always give a one-of-a-kind shopping experience to each customer.

Matt, Rustic Cuff's chief operating officer (COO), was working one of the checkout stations that day. He had about ten people waiting to pay in his line. A woman walked up and slid her credit card under his keyboard, saying, "This is to pay for everything the woman in the scarf is purchasing." The lady quickly walked away, and Matt spotted the woman with the scarf on her head. She was about fifth in his line to check out her selections. After a few minutes the lady was standing before Matt with her own credit card out to pay for cuffs.

Matt greeted her by saying, "Hi, welcome to Rustic Cuff! I know the wait was long, but we so appreciate your coming in today and being willing to wait." She responded, "Oh, it was no problem at all. We had one of the most fun days we've had in a long time!" Matt realized she was with her mother, who chimed in to add, "Today is my daughter's first day out in a while. She's been going through chemotherapy treatment. The weather couldn't have been more perfect to stand in line outside. The chirping birds were such fun to hear! Plus we met some of the best people who were waiting with us, waiting to get inside."

The smiling Matt continued to ring up several cuffs that the woman with the head scarf thought she was purchasing. He then discreetly used the credit card hidden under his keyboard. Matt began boxing each item while the mother and daughter continued to talk to one another. He handed the bag over and, while reaching to touch her hand, said, "I'm also a cancer survivor. Stay strong. I hope you both have a wonderful day." The woman was very moved by Matt's kindness. Suddenly she realized this encouraging man had never taken her money. She started crying and asked, "Who is paying for this?" Matt simply told her, "You have an angel somewhere in the store, and I honestly don't even know who she is."

> "You don't realize what you have done for that lady. You truly made this day perfect for her."

Once the woman could gather her emotions, she insisted Matt convey how thankful she was for such generosity. Matt said he hoped to find the "angel" so he could pass forward her gratefulness. All the while, though, he knew the "angel" would return shortly for her credit card, and the words of the blessed, teary-eyed customer could be relayed to this generous benefactor.

About ten minutes after the cancer survivor and her mother had left, the woman came back up to retrieve her credit card. Matt immediately told her, "You don't realize what you have done for that lady. You truly made this day perfect for her." He went on to tell that this was the first day out of her home in quite a while due to an illness. The woman responded, "Yes, we stood together in line outside and were able to learn quite a lot about one another while waiting. She told me this was her first visit to Rustic Cuff. I wanted to make it a perfect experience for her. I am also a cancer survivor, and she is in the midst of what I've been through in the past. It's a tough road. We shared a lot about never giving up no matter what the circumstance. I wanted her to have whatever she desired in the store. I wanted to do that for her."

This giving woman expected absolutely nothing in return. She simply had made a connection with someone and wanted to give her an exceptional experience in the store. Being the recipient of such generosity is just as extraordinary as this "angel's" own act of kindness.

I didn't hear about it until that afternoon when I saw something posted on Facebook by a woman who shared about an unbelievable experience at the Rustic Cuff showroom. I continued reading and was overjoyed to discover that this woman's entire purchase was anonymously paid for by her "Rustic Cuff angel." I immediately sent out a group text message to everyone who was working that Saturday. I longed to know every detail.

I found out it was Matt who had spoken with both of the women. By the time he finished telling the story to me and others who had gathered, our eyes were filled with tears. Everyone listening was touched deeply because of one act of kindness. What a day at the store. What a connection between two strangers! Kindness is a language that benefited them both—the recipient and the empathetic giver who moved forward to bless her.

❋ ❋ ❋

I shared earlier in the book that one of my goals growing up was to speak Russian fluently. Perhaps it was because most of my friends were learning Spanish and French that I wanted to try something different, something that seemed beyond challenging—and challenging it was. There were very few Russians in Pensacola, Florida, and even fewer at college.

I never had an opportunity to listen to Russians converse. The only conversations I knew of were the ones I read from my textbooks. All of that changed the summer after I graduated from college, the summer spent in Russia. I can't begin to tell you what it felt like to ride on a bus and listen to two people communicate in Russian and know what they were saying!

I understood their language.

I joined in. I asked for directions.

We laughed together.

We shared stories.

We began to understand each other's culture.

All this occurred because I had learned the language of the people. In Russian eyes it was an act of kindness to have an American who had soaked herself in their language and whom they could talk with in a meaningful way. Had I not taken the time to learn their beautiful language, I would have spent the summer depending on a translator. And we all know how much is lost in translation—not so much the words but the emotions. The only thing the Russians may not have been able to understand: I truly received more than I ever gave. They may have forgotten me, but I have never forgotten them.

Shortly after the trip to the country with eleven time zones I read *The Five Love Languages*. The book's author, Gary Chapman, named these as the languages:[1]

- Words of affirmation
- Quality time
- Receiving of gifts
- Acts of service
- Physical touch

I learned that the way I expressed love toward my friends and family was often very different from the way they expressed love back to me. If we judged one another based on our particular idea of what best says, "I love you," if we separated ourselves from people whose love language differed, then nobody would ever be on the same page.

To illustrate, I learned many years ago that my mother-in-law's love language was best expressed through what she marvelously accomplishes in the kitchen. Whenever Terry and I visited my in-laws in Michigan, his mom would spend from sunrise to sunset preparing the most amazing dinner for us. She'd joyfully devote hours putting it together, and it was done with enthusiasm and with love in her heart. Here were her "*ings*" for her darl*ings*:

- Find*ing* the best recipe
- Go*ing* to the grocery store
- Mix*ing*
- Stirr*ing*
- Bak*ing*
- Sett*ing* the table
- Serv*ing* the meal

All of this was done to show us how much we meant to her. I never fully understood. Why would someone spend so much time doing something that could be done in a fraction of the time? Then I learned about love languages, and my eyes were opened. I gained a new understanding that love does not come in one size or shape. I have never had a problem admitting I do not enjoy the kitchen. Terry thinks I would be just fine if our home didn't even have one— which is not true at all because where else would I store Oreos and Oreo ice-cream sandwiches if I had no kitchen? It is true my love language happens not to be found in a room with a stove and a refrigerator. Yes, meals are prepared but usually by Terry as I assist in setting the table or cleaning the dishes. Putting cookbooks in the oven to keep them dust-free sounds like a brilliant idea.

When you discover what language of love someone speaks, then you can learn to express your love for that person in a whole new way. Whereas affection may be the main language of one of your children, another child may speak the language of quality time.

Love does not fit into a particular mold. It is not cookie-cutter. It is its own language. We all speak it slightly differently.

> When you discover what language of love someone speaks, then you can learn to express your love for that person in a whole new way.

We will fall short of enjoying family and friends if we assume they all speak the same language—ours. However, when we take time to carefully observe and listen for their language of love, we will experience aha moments that can change the course of relationships—from struggling to good then maybe from good to great.

The next time you tell someone you love him or her, ask yourself this question: "What language of love does this person speak?" Take the time to learn the person's language whether it's:

- Your child

- Your spouse

- Your mom

- Your dad

- Your sibling

- Your coworker

- Your old friend

Where you felt less than optimistic, where you thought there was no possibility of change, you hopefully will begin to see things in a new light as the words "I love you" take on a whole new meaning.

Chapter 11

PERFECTLY IMPERFECT

I WAS BORN INTO a Jewish family where both my parents' heritage ran deep. My mom became a Christian when I was very young; my dad and the four children followed soon after her.

Yearly, when Christmas arrived, there was not a creature stirring, not even a mouse, not one holiday decoration to be found in our house. This was the scenario for the first eight years of my life. I had no idea what it felt like to celebrate Christmas non-Jewish style with all the festive trappings.

And then in 1979 we moved from Baltimore to the beach city of Pensacola, where I experienced a never-to-be-forgotten Christmas. There was no snow, but the first time I saw the sugar-white sand, it was the whitest snow my brown eyes had ever seen! When our family decided to start celebrating Christmas "with all the trimmings," I happened upon my mom's notebook. She had written all our names down, and four gifts were listed under each name. As each day passed, I kept checking the list to see if something else had been added. One day I noticed my twin brother had six gifts, but the rest of us had only four. Another day one of my siblings had eight! But I had a mom who was always careful to keep every-thing equal among us children.

The number of items kept growing and growing in an attempt to keep the number of gifts the same. When Christmas finally arrived, there were a total of fourteen gifts for each of us. Needless to say, my mom was exhausted by the end of Christmas Day! She had shopped till she dropped, running from one store to the next, returning things to buy them cheaper elsewhere, and was stressed to the max making sure that everything was fair and equal. My dear mom magnificently wrapped seventy-two presents!

Once Christmas morning ended that year, she never wanted to do a repeat of that whole production again. To my parents, cele-brating Hanukkah with one gift every evening for eight nights was looking pretty good once again!

Pat, one of my mom's closest friends, was a professional tree decorator and had done thirty-two theme trees for a large company. The Reamers had never known what it is to have a tree and were clueless about how to string lights, set it up, and so on. Pat insisted on doing all the work for us.

She and Mom spent a couple of hours shopping for the balls, bows, and all kinds of sparkly baubles, with yellow, kelly green, and gold as the color scheme. Then Pat had quite a day, a twelve-hour workday, decorating the huge fake tree with hundreds of lights and the rest of the works. The tree was the most gorgeous one in Pensacola—maybe in the world.

Mom couldn't bear the thought of the labor and time involved in dismantling the magnificent monster as well as the task of wrap-ping up the balls, bows, and baubles. And the thousand lights? *Oy*, not joy, to untangle them next year! Mom, always ripe with ideas, came up with a humdinger of one. My ingenious mother took two bedsheets and wrapped them around the tree, pinning a handwritten sign on the sheets that read "Do not open until December 25!"

Every Christmas, our parents unfurled the sheets, and to our wondering eyes did appear the most gorgeous tree in the world for all to ooh and aah over. The tree was the only decoration other than a few tiny candle lights in our front windows. Every one of my parents' friends and all their children's friends were faced with this sheeted monster twelve months a year. (That tree remained on duty, waiting to be unveiled for seventeen years!)

One year while dating Terry, I joined him at his family home in Michigan for part of the holidays. My oh my! Every inch of the Donovan home was decorated with something outstandingly unique and beautiful! I couldn't believe my eyes when I saw the dancing and singing elves. The Donovans' outside decorations were colorful and carefully placed. The mailbox wasn't forgotten either. The beautiful home fully announced, "Christmas is here!" Bathrooms even had Christmas guest towels.

> If my older Jill could teach my younger Jill anything, it would be that confidence is not what you have. It's who you are.

This was one more life lesson for me. I was taught at a very early age to not judge a book by its cover and to always keep an open mind. This applied to the way people handled celebrating Christmas. I grew up with the bare minimum of decorations, but my husband's family went to a lot of trouble to beautify their home for the holidays. I could be drawn to wrongfully feel my home was imperfect compared with others' homes. Or I could be drawn to wrongfully look down on others who had home decor I thought to be overdone. Pride, self-righteousness, and judgmentalism would've swept over me. My home and its inhabitants weren't perfect by any means, and the same was true of the inhabitants of my husband's home. Perfectly imperfect, all of us!

You might imagine that along with my mother being frugal, she also never subscribed to the idea of name-brand clothing. While all of my friends were wearing Ralph Lauren, Jordache, and IZOD clothes, I wore knockoff shirts with logos clearly showing my clothes were not the brands everyone else was wearing. A Sears logo would have to do.

I'm certain I wasn't alone in feeling the peer pressure in school for the need to keep up with the latest trends. It's easy to fall prey to the line of thinking that you must have and wear whatever everyone else has in order to fit in. If my older Jill could teach my younger Jill anything, it would be that confidence is not what you have. It's who you are, and that it's fine to admire someone else's belongings and beauty as long as it doesn't call your own worth into question.

Well, after a semester of sewing classes in high school I decided to make my own name-brand clothing! I went to the local department store and used my allowance to buy the cheapest thing I could find with an IZOD logo: socks. I went straight home and dug out my mom's sewing machine. I cut the IZOD logo from the socks and stitched the alligator onto a white knockoff polo shirt using my new sewing skills. I could not wait to wear the finished product to school the following week!

Monday came around, as did lunch in the cafeteria. I was talking to Todd, a blossoming crush. He was cracking jokes, and I laughed in an overexaggerated manner at everything he said. Right before the bell rang, Todd told one last joke. I threw my head back in laughter while clapping my hands in front of me. I behaved as if his joke were the funniest thing I had ever heard. My whole body looked to be laughing!

As we started to leave the table, it hit me like a ton of bricks that my sewing skills had not reached the standard I had aimed for. My bracelet got caught on a piece of string, and the alligator was hanging off by two legs. My face was heating up, and I knew it was bright red with embarrassment. Then I blurted out, "Well, I guess they don't make IZOD shirts like they used to!" As my friend was helping me untangle my bracelet from the alligator, he jokingly said, "Oh yeah? I've never had my IZOD logo come off before." He was nice enough not to give me a hard time about my mishap, but I still think Todd knew I had made my own IZOD shirt.

> **It's fine to admire someone else's belongings and beauty as long as it doesn't call your own worth into question.**

I was completely embarrassed leaving the lunchroom. Also, I had been so focused on making sure to laugh at Todd's every joke, lunch had fallen by the wayside. I was starving! So the rest of the day I walked around the hallways and sat in class with a plain white shirt purchased for $7.99, with an alligator fighting for his life to stay attached, all the while counting the minutes until I would be home and could finally eat!

The acceptance Todd and my other friends gave me despite the IZOD fiasco really helped me know that my "imperfections" didn't diminish our friendships. I haven't forgotten that "alligator" day, and it serves me well.

There's one last story I want to share with you that shows how crazy we can be when we get caught up in needing to appear perfect. During my first semester as an adjunct law professor at the University of Tulsa I had an irrational fear. It was that I'd freeze up if students stopped me to ask questions after the lecture—though I may have had the answer on the tip of my tongue. To keep this from happening, I'd walk toward the restroom with my cellphone at my ear as soon as class was over or at the beginning of breaks. Of course no one was on the phone. I was so afraid students would stop me after class to ask questions about the lecture. Please remember, this was my first stint as a professor, and I was a bit nervous, to say the least.

One day, halfway through a three-hour class and when it was almost time for a break, I realized my phone had been left at home. (If Terry spotted my phone at home, he'd wonder how I was surviving without my "third kidney," as he liked to call it.) So during the break I darted out the back door to head for the restroom to avoid questioners.

On my way back to class I tried to appear deep in thought to keep from being interrupted. I walked with my eyes pointed down at my feet and was muttering under my breath as if trying to analyze something in my head. Walking deep in thought must not work as well as a fake phone conversation because I was stopped.

My worst fear came upon me! Two students approached to ask if I had time for a question. Stress enveloped me, and I sure hoped the question might be something like, "What did you have for breakfast?" Needless to report, that was not the question. Instead, they asked a simple question on the statute of limitations, which any first-year law student could have answered. There was no way I, as the professor, could get away with not knowing.

It was as if my brain had gone on a long winter's nap! My memory was not serving me well, so I did not have the answer. I did what anyone would do and created a really good diversion. I exclaimed, "Oh my! I lost my contact. It just fell out of my eye!" The question was forgotten, and the three of us were on the ground searching for my lost contact. Before I knew it, there were five people, and then ten, helping us search. Now I needed to come up with a reason to stop the all-out search for the nonexistent lost contact.

> Embarrassing situations often teach the best lessons;
> they set us free from the impulse to judge wrongly.

The professor (*moi*!) announced, "Wow! I just felt the lens come back into place. It must have somehow slipped to the back of my eye!" I apologized profusely and asked everyone to take his or her seat to continue class. Once the students were seated, I asked Jack, the question guy, to ask again. And now I put my bright idea into play—which was to use the question for a class discussion instead of my stating the answer or having to admit the answer had slipped my mind.

I looked at Lisa, who was sitting next to Jack, and asked, "Lisa, do you know the answer to Jack's question?" She stated the answer, and of course my memory returned. Lisa was correct. At that point the rest of the class was back in the room and ready to start the second half of the lecture. I was more than delighted to start as well but still wanted to avoid any more questions I may or may not be prepared to answer.

All three of these stories are great reminders not to take myself too seriously. Embarrassing situations often teach the best lessons; they set us free from the impulse to judge wrongly. Humility creates a greater empathy for others, as it enables us to relate to people when we recall the times we were flustered.

If I am conducting a meeting with a group of people who don't yet know one another, I like to start off by asking each person to share his or her most embarrassing moment. This seems to put us all on a level playing field and remove any self-righteousness we may have brought into a boardroom. It's also amazing how laughter is the great icebreaker, and hearing others' stories is yet further confirmation that all of us are far from perfect…yet in God's eyes we are *perfectly* imperfect.

Chapter 12

RANDOM IS NEVER TRULY RANDOM

SOMETIMES GIVING TO other people can be hard and awkward. But regardless of the occasional uneasy moments I want to follow my "knower" when I feel led to do something. Many times the prompting is to gift a complete stranger.

Terry and the girls were out of town recently, and I had the rare occasion of a weekend alone at our house. It was uneventful, which is nice every once in a while! By the time Sunday rolled around, I was definitely ready for the normal banter, laughter, and singing to fill our home once again. That morning, for the first time, I walked into church alone and slid into a seat in the side section. To the right of me was a couple I did not know—we smiled at one another.

Our pastor started his sermon, which was based on the importance of giving even during tough economic times. He began to talk about giving back something even when we didn't feel like it or when there wasn't much to give. In the middle of the message, it hit me. (By this point I had come to recognize this feeling as one of those hard-to-ignore promptings.) My heart was telling me to gift the couple next to me with whatever money I had in my purse. Believe me, I argued with the prompting for the next fifteen minutes—not because I didn't want to give whatever money was in my handbag but because of a dilemma: How am I going to move ahead with God's leading? This giving gesture might prove to be a bit uncomfortable. However, I've learned it's far better to be inconvenienced than to be disobedient.

> Sometimes giving to other people can be hard and awkward. But regardless of the occasional uneasy moments I want to follow my "knower" when I feel led to do something.

Now that I knew I was going to follow the prodding to gift them with money, I wondered how to carry it out. I lifted my purse off the floor and put it on my lap, wanting to casually look inside for some money. I generally don't carry cash since my preference is to use a debit/credit card because it's simpler for me. I began digging doubtfully in the bottom of my purse, as if I were looking for a tissue, yet with the hope there would be maybe a five- or ten-dollar bill. With eyes focused on the pastor, my fingers felt a bill of some sort. I was so happy to now be able to follow through with the prompting.

I wrapped my hand around the cash and set my purse back down on the floor. I didn't want to attract attention with what I was getting ready to do. I needed a stealth idea to come to mind so I could drop the money in the woman's purse without her seeing me. As the sermon continued, my mind wandered, "How can I pull this off? What if she looks down and sees my hand by her purse and thinks I am taking something from her? That is a scene I would like to avoid, especially in church!"

Finally garnering the courage to just go for it, I took a bracelet off my wrist and wrapped it around the bill. Adding a little weight to it might keep it from falling out of her leather bag. I quickly glanced down at the bill to see what it was, and much to my surprise it was Benjamin Franklin. I had no idea there was a one-hundred-dollar bill in my purse and was scratching my head as to how I couldn't recall it being there. At that moment I decided not to ask why, how, what, or when. I held the bracelet with the tucked bill in my palm and reached down to my shoe, as if I were fixing something on it. As I leaned over, with a quickly beating heart, I slipped the money into an opening in her purse.

When the service ended, we stood up and introduced ourselves, and the couple and I began chatting with one another. I learned some things about them and truly enjoyed our ten-minute conversation as we walked out to our cars.

Later that evening Terry and the girls were back home, and all the normal sounds filled the house again. I opened my laptop to answer a few emails and found one from the woman who sat beside me at church. Tears poured down my cheeks as I read her story. When I got to the last part, a wave of gratitude swept over me for the grace that enabled me to obey—though it involved a rather awkward move. Here's how the woman ended:

> Although we have always wanted to tithe, we never had. We lived like a lot of people, in the "red zone"—paycheck to paycheck, kind of robbing Peter to pay Paul. So Sunday as Alex was preaching, I just felt like God was telling me, "You can do this; have faith and trust Me!" As I continued to listen to Alex, while having this internal discussion with God, I was trying to figure out how to make it work and honestly was scared. As we got in the car after church and I looked in my

purse, I just cried! I knew it was God telling me to trust Him, and everything would be fine!

Skeptics would call what happened coincidental, just a lucky chance encounter. Of the hundreds of seats I could have chosen in the large auditorium, I wound up next to one hand-selected couple. I know this was not random; all along that seat was waiting just for me. That special place, in the side section on the aisle, turned out to bless and touch my heart in more ways than it did the couple's.

May we all continue to be moved by the promptings of our "knowers" and remember that even though a seat may appear to be random, it never truly is.

Here's another story that reminds me that with God the random things are never random. Late one night I was ready for bed but decided to see if there were any posts to respond to. I saw a post by a young woman named Jackie, writing about her life as a military wife living overseas. Jackie and her family had been living in Seoul, South Korea, for the previous two and a half years. She was expressing how much she missed her family back in the United States.

Jackie and her husband had two young children, the youngest being born after they moved to Seoul. She could not wait until her parents could finally meet their new grandchild. Mentioning that money was tight and the flights were astronomical, they had no plans to be back in the United States for another year.

At the end of her post Jackie told a story about a Rustic Cuff bracelet her mother had recently shipped to her. That day she felt compelled to give her mother's gift away to a friend who had confided about her own struggles. Jackie posted this to encourage others to do something nice for someone else. Even in the midst of her own struggles she wanted to spread the word that happiness comes from serving others. Even though she was having a hard day and missing her family, she was able to find joy when she gifted her cuff to someone else.

As I read Jackie's story, I started thinking of the airline miles I had accrued over the past few years. I knew I had built up some miles from using certain credit cards for business but hadn't looked at one of them for a while. Minutes before going on Facebook that night, I randomly (or not so randomly) decided to check how many miles there were in case I wanted to use them for an upcoming trip. I was shocked to find more than I anticipated and thought, "How in the world am I ever going to use all of these miles?" Then, in God's perfect timing, this woman's Facebook post appeared, and I wanted to help this family reunite. The "knower" was working once again.

It was the middle of the night in Tulsa, but it was daytime in Seoul, so I sent Jackie a private message, hoping she would see it and we could talk a bit. She did see it, so we talked about her life in Tulsa and all her travels since marrying her military husband. While she missed her family back home, she could find joy in her journey across the world. Jackie knew she would never have seen all the beautiful places they had visited if her husband were not serving. She added that her life was not just about finding joy through her travels but that she focused each day on doing something nice for someone else. Not only was she doing something for another person, but she was making her own day a little brighter in the process.

Jackie told me of her own cuffs and which one she had given away that afternoon. I promised to send her that very cuff the next day to replace the one she had gifted. We had made a genuine connection, and my "knower" reinforced my feelings to offer her family a round-trip flight back to Tulsa. This way they could visit her parents.

When I offered my airline miles to her, she was astonished but accepted the gift. Over the next few days we stayed in contact so I could book the flights for her using the miles. I made her promise to contact me while she was in Tulsa, and she did. We met at my office, and Jackie came in with her sweet family. They were all so grateful to be together, and her mom and dad were able to finally meet their youngest grandchild. It was Jackie and her husband's anniversary that weekend, and it was going to be the first time they had ever been able to go out on their actual anniversary alone since having their girls.

What felt random—she and I connecting that night over the internet—was really not random at all. Our paths were supposed to intersect. There was nothing coincidental about her post at that exact time and my discovery of the unused airline miles just before that. It was an intersection that God had intended all along.

This last "random" story shows the way God planned ahead to put the right message on the right cuff for the right person at the right time. Recently Terry and I went to hear vocalist Sandi Patty in concert. Of course Sandi was amazing, as she always is. Afterward we went to dinner with some friends. At the end of our meal we were sitting at the table wondering why the check hadn't arrived yet. The service was excellent, but the check seemed to be taking a long time. When the waiter came back to our table, he said our check had been "taken care of" by another person. We persisted in asking him who paid for our dinner, but he would not say because the other patron had requested to remain unknown.

I didn't want to leave the restaurant without thanking the person who paid for our meal, so I asked for the manager. It wouldn't hurt to try one more time to find out who had been so generous. The manager had the same answer. This person wanted to remain anonymous. As she was explaining why she could not say who paid for our dinner, her eyes seemed to wander to a specific table with three women. Little did the manager know her unspoken language clued me in to who the person might be.

I went to their table to introduce myself, and I simply said, "Thank you."

Holding back a smile, one of the women responded, "For what?"

I answered, "For the delicious Cobb salad I just ate and for making our day."

Realizing they had been found out, one of the women said she wanted to pay for our meal as a gesture of thanks. She went on to tell of a recent visit to one of the stores, where she went to select something for her daughter who had, sadly, just experienced a miscarriage. The woman was helped by one of the showroom girls, Debbie, who was so touched by the story she gifted the selected bracelet. This lady felt so blessed by Debbie's kind act that on noticing Terry and me at a table, she wanted to silently say thank you.

The three ladies began telling me of some of their favorite quote cuffs, and I looked down, remembering there were exactly three quote cuffs on my wrists. I felt they were no longer mine. I distinctly remembered pulling the cuffs out of my drawer earlier that night, thinking I'd find someone to gift them to. I was compelled to hand two of them to the women on either side of me.

I looked at the third lady, who was sitting directly across the table, and thought about the last cuff on my wrist. My heart sank.

Since we had just been talking about her daughter's miscarriage, the remaining quote was far from appropriate. But what choice did I have?

> **When you learn to live fully in the moment—as random as it may seem—with no full understanding of the *why*, that's when true freedom occurs.**

With high hopes that somehow the words on the cuff had magically changed, I slowly removed it from my arm. Staring at the words, I had to read them three times. The quote said, "Never give up." How was this possible? The only quote I'd ever put on this one particular style bracelet was "Expect Nothing. Appreciate Everything."

Then a very distant memory came back that the very first sample I made for this style cuff was designed with a different quote: "Never give up." Somehow when I reached in the drawer that morning, it was that one-of-a-kind cuff I happened to put on. As the woman took it, she immediately started to cry and gave me the tightest hug imaginable. I knew for certain this was nothing less than one more providential surprise.

As we begin to look back at certain people we've met or places we've been to, we discover that what appeared completely random to us at the moment was never truly by chance at all. Our steps were ordered before we ever knew where the path was headed. I encourage you to follow the leading in your heart, your "knower," in every situation—even when you can't see the purpose. When you learn to live fully in the moment—as random as it may seem—with no full understanding of the *why*, that's when true freedom occurs.

Chapter 13

BE ALL THERE

M ATT GRIFFIN, NOW a dear friend as well as COO, was
diagnosed with stage-three colon cancer on December
13, 2005. By God's grace and by strong determination
he is healthy and well today. Recently we were talking about his
experiences during chemotherapy and radiation treatments, and I
was curious how he handled each day of the treatment. More specifically I wanted to know how he was able to cope emotionally.

I asked him, "Did you have a calendar that counted down each
day until the treatments were complete?" I could just picture something hanging above his desk that he would glance at to see how
many days or weeks were left of what he describes as "the most difficult days of my life."

Matt experienced a lack of energy and exhaustion that was
almost unbearable and even told the doctor he didn't want to continue treatment once his first round was over. After hearing about
the physical exhaustion, lack of energy, and overall general pain, I
could see why Matt, or anyone else, would want the days of treatment to go by as quickly as possible. In the beginning he would

focus on the total number of weeks and days remaining and would wish the days away to reach the "end of that treatment" and then circle it on the calendar as fast as he could.

Matt knew this was no way to live and realized that living for a future over which he had no control was a futile effort. By putting the future Friday's worries into his Monday, he was robbed of today's joys, along with being less productive. He saw how much of each day was being missed and that he would never be able to get back the time wasted. He gave all those cares to God, and with a new mind-set to live fully in the present, the weight of the future lifted.

With this profound change Matt mentally stopped looking behind or ahead, but he also made an actual physical change—to his vehicle. One day, after buckling his two young boys in the car, he found himself worrying about the future. Matt imagined not being able to see his boys every day if the treatments proved unsuccessful. What would life be like for them if their dad wasn't around to help raise them? He brought to mind the grace already given to change his thoughts and chose to move his thoughts from the future to living for today, in the moment. When he buckled his own seatbelt, he silently repeated he would only think on today, not the past or the future.

> To "fully live" only when the sun is shining means we would miss out on half of our lives.

Then Matt did something symbolic to help him always remember his focus; he reached for the rearview mirror. He pointed the mirror away from the back window and adjusted it so the mirror was pointed to his boys in the back seat. He did not need to see what was going on behind his vehicle, but he did need to see the faces of his two young boys. They were five and three at the time, and Matt wanted the constant reminder of how bright a future they had ahead of them. If there was a car behind them, he would just look over his shoulder to find out. His boys were more important than not having the discomfort of turning around to look backward. And who cares what is behind you anyway?

There will always be an ebb and flow of clouds and sunshine throughout our lives. To "fully live" only when the sun is shining means we would miss out on half of our lives. Sometimes it is hard to catch this truth, but it really helps to remind ourselves, even if it's a hundred times a day at first, to let go of yesterday's regrets. One more major reminder: we have no control over our tomorrows.

There is another matter that frequently causes us not to be present in our lives. This is the matter of technology. We feel pressured to stay in touch with work, friends, and family through email and other electronic means. To be honest, we all have some sort of obsession with these electronic devices that can inhibit our ability to be fully present at any given moment.

Some of the most precious memories with my children include times when there was no way to charge my phone or times on road trips when there was no phone service.

A few of my daughters' fondest memories were made either when my phone was on the fritz or when the girls lost the privilege to use their own devices for a period of time.

When free from constantly checking the insistent phones, we get to taste what it was like twenty years ago, before there

were any of these trappings. At first it seems stressful to be disconnected electronically, but then the stress soon turns into a feeling
of freedom, allowing us to fully live and take in the moment. We
are released from ties to iPads, computers, and smartphones! Gone
are the obligatory feelings to be available at any given moment.

One family vacation we decided to stay at a hotel located in the
middle of the desert. Of course as we were arriving at the hotel in
the middle of nowhere, I realized my cell phone battery was close
to 15 percent. Digging through my bag, and doing it again, and
then again, I came up with... no cord. I knew the "must-have" wire
would suddenly appear out of nowhere, but it never did. I had no
charger! Normally this wouldn't be a huge problem. I could use one
of the girls' or Terry's, but I had just purchased a new phone, and
the charger was completely different from the ones used for their
phones.

I asked the concierge if he could locate the correct charger for
me, but the runner had already made his last run to "town" that
day. I was told, "Rest assured, the courier will be back within
forty-eight hours, and we will have him bring the charging cord
for you." Terry looked at me and whispered, "What are we going
to do without your third kidney?" (Remember, my "third kidney" is
Terry's loving way of referring to my phone.) I laughed and blew it
off as if not having my phone for a few days were no big deal. There
was no way I was going to give in and show how uncomfortable it
was for me not being able to connect to the outside world.

After only a few hours had passed, I realized there was a sense
of freedom and relief. Not checking my phone every few minutes to
make sure I wasn't missing something was good for me. I actually
started enjoying being disconnected and being all there with my
family in the middle of the desert. I was present in every activity,
whether we were doing a puzzle, swimming, hiking, or just being
lazy in the room together.

When the courier did arrive with the charging cord, I made a promise I would only allow myself thirty minutes in the morning and thirty minutes at night to look at my phone for the rest of the trip. (I may have stayed in the bathroom a little longer than normal, however.)

I learned several things while I was disconnected from the online world. One is that you can actually survive being disconnected! Two, you might actually thrive! I found myself more cognizant of my family's needs and the needs of some of the staff working at the resort. This allowed me to be fully present and aware of the needs of those around me and to show unexpected kindness. The joy I felt was magnified knowing that I made a difference in someone's day.

Today we can still enjoy all the available technologies. It just takes some effort on our part to make a conscious decision to lay down the device in order to "be all there."

Chapter 14

FAITH IN GOD INCLUDES FAITH IN HIS TIMING

NOT LONG AGO I was asked to speak to a marketing class at a local high school in Tulsa. At the end of the discussion on marketing ideas I talked about kindness and the impact giving to others can have. Toward the end of my time there, I gave each student a challenge and left the classroom. Each student was handed a fifty-dollar bill with a challenge to find a stranger to give the money to. The recipient had to be a stranger. My desire was for the students to learn to listen to their "knower" and experience what it's like to give to someone without knowing who, where, or what the money would be used for.

About a month after I gave them the challenge, I was contacted by one of the students' mothers. She asked if she could meet me in person to thank me. Being intrigued, of course I said, "Yes, let's meet!" When we met, the first thing the mother expressed was that I would not believe the impact "the challenge" had on her son,

Jason. She then went on to tell me the entire story of the changes she had seen in him.

The afternoon Jason came home with the fifty-dollar bill, he proceeded to tell her the whole story of the challenge. At dinner that night they discussed various ways he could gift the money and which way might have the greatest impact. He made a decision to give the money to a local Catholic charity. The two made a list of the different places to which he could donate. After dinner Jason asked his mom if they could drive to these charities in hopes of giving the money away that night.

As they were driving, the mom said she was secretly hoping he would find someone soon since the sun was going down and they were not in the best part of town to be driving around aimlessly at night. She saw many different people walking along the street, some who were probably homeless. The mom hoped he would feel prompted to give one of these people the money so they could return home. She didn't want to influence Jason or rush him, so she said nothing. A few minutes later he said, "I'm not feeling anything, so let's head back to the house."

The next day after school Jason walked in the door a bit frustrated. Some of the students from the marketing class had already given away their money, and he couldn't figure out why he hadn't been led to do the same. His mom reassured him that it would happen and to remember his "knower," his heart, would lead him to just the right person. And then it happened!

The following day Jason went to a convenience store after school. He spotted a woman in a vehicle feeding her infant from a milk carton. The window was lowered a bit, allowing him to hand the woman the fifty-dollar bill. At that moment the woman's husband came from the store to the car, asking what was going on. Jason simply said he wanted to give the fifty-dollar bill to them. The father was incredibly grateful and told Jason he worked across the

street at a fast-food restaurant and wouldn't be paid until the following week. Sadly they had no money to buy food for the baby or
themselves.

Jason's mom told me the story didn't end there. "My son is an
Eagle Scout who recently finished a service project. Donations had
come in, which enabled him to complete it. He had some unused
funds that were not needed for the project. My son visited with
his scoutmaster, telling him the story about the challenge given in
the marketing class. He explained how the challenge had greatly
changed him. Jason wanted to do more."

The mom continued by telling me her son asked the scoutmaster
if he could donate the money left over from his project to a Catholic
charity. The scoutmaster suggested Jason go to the donors to check
with them. Of course everyone said, "Great!" The following day he
went to a charity and gave the donation.

I was in awe of this mother's story. She was amazed to see her
young son so transformed. She went on to say Jason wanted to go
even further with giving to others. While she sat at dinner with him
recently, the whole "challenge" experience opened the door for the
mother to share the concept of giving. Jason went on to say that this
challenge resonated so deeply that he wanted to take a certain per-
centage out of every paycheck to donate to charity. The mom told
me, "He has a passion and a need to do this. Jason's already a great
eighteen-year-old, but this challenge made him into so much more."

The mother finished by saying her changed son was now
thinking about other people and the impact he could have on them
with his giving.

Trusting God's timing was a lesson I had struggled with (and fought
my way through) years before I was talking about it in local schools.

On graduation day from Oral Roberts University I was so happy to be finished and to begin living in the real world! Terry and I had been dating for a while and had planned to get engaged and marry at some point after we finished school. Terry had graduated early from ORU and moved back to his hometown in Michigan while I finished my senior year. I was excited knowing Terry was coming for my special day.

The following day, after celebrating, Terry had a somber look on his face and said he needed to tell me something before we moved further in our relationship. It sounded ominous; I could not imagine what he needed to tell me, but then he shared that while he was home, he was diagnosed with Hodgkin's disease.

With this new diagnosis everything in Terry's life changed. He changed too. With his determination to be cured of Hodgkin's, our plans to have a life together were put on the back burner. Sometimes I would become frustrated and say to myself, "Are we ever going to be married?"

> Regardless of all the negative circumstances against you, if you have hope, it supersedes anything standing in the way of your desires.

Then I had a specific dream that changed my outlook. In this dream I saw a family photo so detailed I even remember what the frame looked like. Everyone was in the picture. It was Mom and Dad, my three brothers, and me. In the back of the photo I saw Terry standing there. He wasn't standing with us; instead, he was standing in the distance by himself. When I woke up, I was puzzled as to the meaning of the dream. Then I knew Terry was going to be in the picture. He would *always* be in the picture, literally and figuratively.

This dream was a thread to hold on to. As I think back on this dream, I knew God was showing me everything was going to work out, yet I was to remain in a holding pattern during that time. I was supposed to sit tight even if it didn't fit my own timing. Terry went through a grueling regimen of treatment, and as of this day he remains cancer-free. We are grateful to God for his good health.

Not long after that dream Terry asked me to marry him, and that's what we happily did. In the end getting married affirmed the practice of having hope and faith. I continue hoping for things not seen. I know there will be trials in my life, but there will always be great hope.

If I did allow myself to worry and fret, then those fearful feelings would wind up filling the space where hope belongs. Worrying adds no benefit, but hope does. When you know you're holding something in your heart that is supposed to be part of your life, then you can know God put the desire inside for a reason. Regardless of all the negative circumstances against you, if you have hope, it supersedes anything standing in the way of your desires.

After I learned to wait for God's timing to marry Terry, I still struggled to trust His timing. He wasn't through teaching me this lesson.

Since I was a little girl, having children and a family of my own was one of my dreams. When playing house as a child, I always played the role of the mother, and my friends were my babies. It never once occurred to me I might have trouble becoming pregnant. I later learned this was going to be a season in my life when my faith in God's timing would bring me through a storm.

Terry and I joyfully wed, and when we decided to start a family, my dream of being a mother was actually going to become a reality. The day I discovered I was pregnant, my excitement poured out all over the place! There was no reason to think my pregnancy would not be normal. But this changed one day when I knew something was very wrong during my last exam for the semester in law school. Later that day I miscarried. No words can describe how upset I was. My imagination already had run its full course, picturing what life was going to look like with a baby.

One night I had a dream I can clearly remember to this day. In the dream I saw a toddler about two or three years old. I woke up having no clue what it meant, but it gave me a sense of hope. I held the image of the little child close—very close—to my heart. Eventually I became pregnant again and had my first daughter, Ireland, with no complications. When she was born, the dream came back to mind right away. The baby I had dreamed of looked identical to Ireland! She was my baby all along, and it worked out according to His plan. I saw then that the Lord's timing is perfect. Now I look back at the dream and know God intended for me to have this precious child all along. He had spoken in the still of the night—even showing me what she would look like. In actuality that amazing dream greatly helped to relieve any anxiety during my pregnancy.

When Ireland was a few years old, Terry and I decided we wanted another child. I became pregnant fairly quickly but found myself constantly on edge. The prior miscarriage, before Ireland's birth, seemed to hang over me. One day there was an odd pain in my calf, so I went to the doctor to have it checked out. He also did a quick checkup on the baby since I was already there. The doctor discovered I had an ectopic pregnancy, and soon after that I miscarried for the second time.

At this point I was full of fear about pregnancy and losing my babies. Then I found out I was expecting again. It had been a year since the ectopic pregnancy, and my doctor wanted to do an examination right away. To my devastation we found out that this too was an ectopic pregnancy.

Despite these losses, which brought us sorrow, I never lost my desire to have another child. One morning a pregnancy test showed I was having another baby! The nine months of this pregnancy were problem-free, and the priceless outcome was my little girl August. We actually used the nickname Peanut when she was a baby, and it stuck. She is still Peanut! With Ireland, Peanut, and Terry, I knew my family was complete, and God knew the plan all along. He intended for me to have these exact two girls, and I believe God's timing is never off.

- Faith can be difficult to hold on to, especially faith in God's timing. It doesn't always make logical sense, but it is always worth trusting.

- Faith is not knowing if anyone will show up to help you build but building anyway. Faith is knowing you will get what you need when you need it and not a day too late.

- Faith believes in something when your own reason is screaming, "No!" When everything else is pointing to a no, faith whispers, "Yes."

Every morning when we wake, we have the choice to follow one of two roads. It is as if we are standing at a crossroads, and we get to decide which road to travel. We can select the road of anxiety or the road of faith. The road of anxiety is covered in fear and doubt. Or we can choose to have faith—that is, to trust God. The more we exercise the faith muscle, the easier it gets.

> Faith can be difficult to hold on to, especially faith in God's timing. It doesn't always make logical sense, but it is always worth trusting.

The next time things are foggy, take to heart what one of my favorite authors, Corrie ten Boom, said: "Faith is like a radar which sees through the fog."[1] Remember, the outcome might not always be exactly as we've pictured it, but we can know that God has us. His plan for us is always perfect.

Chapter 15

JUST BREATHE

THERE ARE SEVERAL of our quote cuffs that we cannot seem to make fast enough. Could it be that particular sayings resonate with a greater number of people? Yes, for sure. Some quotes seem to help people no matter where they find themselves in life. One of the top three quotes is "Just Breathe"—a necessity for every living person.

We can go weeks without food.

We can go days without water.

We can survive only minutes without breathing.

We breathe thousands of times a day without even thinking about it. Breathing is not only important for our bodies but also a necessity to truly live life well—to live freely.

Why would we need a reminder to do something our bodies do naturally? That's because certain situations cause us to hold our breath. Days full of anxiety will do this—both literally and figuratively. In extremely stressful times we may find ourselves walking around in a constant state of hyperventilation.

I remember Terry and I attending a Lamaze class before the birth of our first daughter, Ireland. One of the main focuses in class had to do with breathing during labor pains. In my early thirties at this time, I had rarely in my entire life given any thought to breathing. The Lamaze instructor taught me how to breathe correctly during delivery.

Guess what I did the moment I felt the first contraction pain?

Yes, I held my breath.

Not only was it a natural reaction, but everything I learned in class went out the window the moment I felt pain. I forgot my lessons. I forgot about the benefit of breathing during labor pains—it causes more oxygen to flow through the blood. This action releases endorphins, which bring a calming effect. I forgot that breathing enables a woman to focus and be more present, which was something I greatly wanted in this moment—a moment I had anticipated for so long, a moment I had feared may never come. When those initial hard labor pains came, I put nothing into practice my Lamaze instructor taught.

Until someone gently reminded me: "Just breathe."

Now, don't get me wrong. It wasn't as if the pain left the moment I started breathing. It was that I could manage the pain. When I held my breath, it literally felt as if I were underwater, but when I decided to breathe, I lost the feeling of suffocation. And I could begin to *see and appreciate* the miracle of a child coming into this world again.

A while back an IV was needed for some tests my doctor wanted to run. I had been short of breath one night while I was sleeping, and he wanted to get to the bottom of it. When the nurse inserted the IV, a vein blew during the insertion of the tiny needle. I had never had that experience, and it created a bit of a panic in me—I didn't even know blowing a vein was a thing! But let me tell you, I know *all* about it now.

> **Breathing is essential not only to living but also to living well. Choose to just breathe, not only when things are going well but also when times are tough.**

Since that morning I have had three more IVs. When I walked into the room where the "needle nurse" stood waiting for me, all naïveté had disappeared as to what may happen. I was fully aware because of the previous experience. Honestly I half expected it to happen every time. When I got the third IV, the nurse looked into my squinted eyes and said, "You are not breathing. I need you to breathe. Let's bring some color back to your face."

I made a decision that morning I was no longer going to *expect* the worst when I walked into the room with all the IV paraphernalia. Expecting the worst from the little needle was taking my breath away. And losing my breath was taking away my ability to think clearly.

I decided to breathe.

I decided to pray.

I decided to keep myself open despite any previous experiences. Vulnerability is a freeing attitude.

Breathing is essential not only to living but also to living well. Choose to *just breathe*, not only when things are going well but also when times are tough—*especially* when times are tough. And with every breath during troublesome times ask God to replace the cynicism with wisdom. And the anxiety with peace. And the helplessness with hope. Stand back and watch as you just breathe, because He will answer. He does every time.

I'm remembering the summer when on a family vacation the four of us decided to sign up for an exercise class. You've heard the expression "It's up in the air"—this form of exercise was literally practiced up in the air. The first question that came to my mind was the obvious—"Why?"—to which my youngest daughter, Peanut, answered, "Why not?"

About ten minutes into learning how to move my body into positions it did not even know it could do, our instructor looked at me and softly encouraged me with, "Jill, don't forget to breathe. You're holding your breath."

I couldn't help but think, "Well, of course I'm holding my breath! I'm terrified I'll fall out of this piece of silk while my body is bent backward, forward, and sideways all at the same time. What was I thinking when I agreed to this?"

The instructor told me to inhale as deeply as I could, hold my breath for a second, and then exhale slowly. Then she asked me to do it again. And again.

> We all can understand it is fine and natural for us as humans to contract and curl up when hit with unexpected, unwelcome news that brings emotional pain. It's what you do with the pain, and how you work through it, that counts.

After the third time my head suddenly cleared. I gained a little bit of confidence. This allowed me to consider that what she was asking was within the realm of possibility. I was able to separate myself from the fear of falling on my face during the minutes I was *hanging* from this silk attached to the ceiling.

I gained all this from *just breathing*!

Choose to *just breathe*, which is easy to do when things are going well, but we should also make this choice when times are tough—*especially when times are tough.*

Here are some additional helpful thoughts on the subject. They may be repeating some of what you've already seen in this chapter, but because "Just Breathe" is a popular bracelet, this subject may bear repeating in order to digest it well.

Let's imagine you are taking a walk. You are enjoying every-thing about this walk: the flowers, the birds, the person's hand you are holding.

You haven't a care in the world…until you unexpectedly stub your toe.

You didn't see the bump or the rock in the road, so you stumble, or maybe even fall.

What do you do? You immediately tighten up. You ignore the daffodils, you hear the chickadees no longer, you let go of that warm hand, and *you focus on the pain.* You might even hold your breath for a couple of seconds.

The freedom and openness you experienced right up to that very moment was replaced by a small level of cautiousness, an extra cover, a mental padding. Your first thoughts may be:

- "I certainly won't allow this to happen again."

- "I feel better with this extra layer of padding on me."

- "With padding if someone or something hurts me in the future, I will be ready."

- "With padding I won't feel things as sharply or as deeply."

- "God knows my heart certainly cannot handle ever being this vulnerable again."

In reality, though, you are no longer being the *real* you, the one who used to breathe deeply and freely. The one who lived without extra layers of caution. The uncynical you. It's as if you begin to see the world through the eyes of a person who simply expects to get hurt instead of someone who uses wisdom when making choices—yet is open and free. We all can understand it is fine and natural for us as humans to contract and curl up when hit with unexpected, unwelcome news that brings emotional pain. It's what you do with the pain, and how you work through it, that counts. We have two choices:

1. Continue to either take short breaths or hold your breath in anticipation of the next negative moment that is going to happen in your life. Become skeptical of each new person who enters your life. Stay closed off to anything positive that tries to enter your world. "After all," you may tell yourself, "why wouldn't this end up just like the last situation or person that did me harm?"

2. Choose to breathe. Breathe through the pain, not just taking short breaths to get by. Instead, with every inhaled breath and exhaled breath remind yourself that this life is not a perfect one by any means. Good things happen to bad people, and bad things happen to very good people.

> The authenticity of your life depends on whether you choose to continue to breathe during the hurt and pain.

Say to yourself, "God didn't intend for me to shrivel up and stop living. He created me for *life*, and holding my breath brings the opposite. Living life closed off and cynical is not truly living at all." Figuratively speaking, if we hold our breath, it's true we may not feel the pain as deeply, but we will certainly be devoid of the joy of living.

The authenticity of your life depends on whether you choose to continue to breathe during the hurt and pain. You can react to emotional, mental, or physical pain by contracting and hiding, or you can choose to breathe through it—one breath at a time—without fear of what or who is going to hurt you next.

Chapter 16

GRACE CHANGES EVERYTHING

EVERYONE HAS A story.

Some people walk around with their storybooks wide open, and you can see exactly what chapter and page of their journey they are on. Others keep their books closed, and you only see the covers. Whether the covers are worn or whether they look brand new—well taken care of—you truly have no idea where they are in their stories. It has been my experience that the people with the hardest shells, with the toughest exteriors, are usually the ones who have some pretty problematic pages in their stories. There are some chapters they never thought they would make it out of. These are the people who need the most grace.

Grace bridges gaps that from all appearances look too wide to ever be crossed. Growing up I thought grace was only something we said before each meal. Later I learned grace is much more than a prayer; grace is undeserved favor, a gift that cannot be earned. I have experienced the magnitude of God's grace despite the many times I have disappointed Him. These experiences have changed me. Understanding grace gives me the freedom to not judge, or to not decide what I think others deserve. I now let God deal with the hearts of those who offend me.

We frankly have no idea what burdens others may be bearing, and it's not our place to decide if they are worthy of our forgiveness. Our place is to give grace regardless. Everybody is hurting somewhere inside. We may never know the backstory to someone's actions, and that's OK. We want to forgive others in our hearts even when they are not sorry—maybe *especially* when they are not sorry.

Showing grace teaches us it's not our responsibility to right the wrong but to leave that to the One we all will answer to in the end. We hold the keys of grace and forgiveness that replace bitterness and pain with freedom and new joy. Remember, learning to show grace is a daily process. Before we know it, that grace will bridge the gap we thought was permanent.

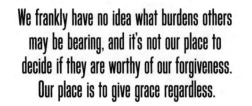

We frankly have no idea what burdens others may be bearing, and it's not our place to decide if they are worthy of our forgiveness. Our place is to give grace regardless.

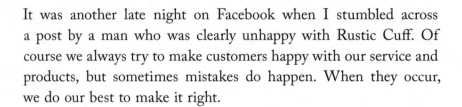

It was another late night on Facebook when I stumbled across a post by a man who was clearly unhappy with Rustic Cuff. Of course we always try to make customers happy with our service and products, but sometimes mistakes do happen. When they occur, we do our best to make it right.

This post was different, though. It seemed as if the man had never purchased anything. He couldn't believe people would stand in line in the cold just for a bracelet and stated his wife would not receive any Rustic Cuff bracelets for Christmas because he could not understand all the hype.

I cringed the entire time I read his post. I knew if he made it into one of the stores, his outlook would probably change. (Our goal in the showroom is to create a one-of-a-kind experience for each and every person.) This man simply wasn't aware that it's not about the bracelets but about the camaraderie that comes with being part of Rustic Cuff. That is, he wasn't aware *yet...*

This perplexed man received a private message from me letting him know I would love to meet with him at the showroom. It was right before Christmas, but he made time to meet me anyway. When he came in, I assured him I completely understood why he would be baffled about the long lines of people. I gently offered, "Rustic Cuff is truly not about the bracelets."

Waiting for him was a box I'd prepared as a gift for him so he could surprise his wife at Christmas, but then I decided I wanted him to actually experience the showroom instead. Maybe then the man would understand what I tried to explain. I asked him to pick out anything he wanted and told him it was a gift. As he was about to leave my office, I handed him two gift cards, each for two hundred dollars. I asked him to find two people waiting in line to give the cards to.

He went outside to the line, and when he came back inside, I could see his eyes were red and he was holding back tears. The man had found two girls about the age of his own daughter and gave the gift cards to them. Not only did his perception of a company that made bracelets change that day, but he said he would forever be grateful for the experience of impacting another's life that day in a way that probably touched him more than it did them. I was beyond happy that I was able to show him the true purpose of this company.

The man's next post on Facebook had a different tone. He thanked me for showing him the meaning behind Rustic Cuff and expressed his gratitude for the employees, who created a shopping experience he'd never had before. The man wrote it as if we were all old friends instead of having just met, and we all felt the same. Giving the two girls the gift cards and seeing their eyes light up like a Christmas tree was a real blessing to him. The whole experience was a magical moment for everyone involved with Rustic Cuff that day. Extending grace to this complaining man transformed his outlook, his attitude. And I learned one more time how invaluable showing grace is.

I was out of town with my family when one day another Facebook post caught my attention. The post was made by a woman who wrote that Rustic Cuff is stupid and that anyone can make these bracelets, even her elementary-aged daughter. I continued reading and saw that other women were also commenting on her post with messages of the same type. It seemed to be never-ending, and each comment made me sense the negativity would spread like wildfire.

In my mind I knew this was going to be disastrous, but I didn't know what to do. Being out of town and unable to invite them to meet me at the showroom presented a challenge. Instead, I decided to comment on her post and tagged each person who had made a negative comment. I invited them to visit the showroom so we could connect in person. One by one each woman who said something negative about Rustic Cuff showed up at a different time, and once we met face-to-face, something changed. It was getting together in a personal, gracious way that changed attitudes. They were each surprised when I gave them a special gift after we met and chatted.

When it was all said and done, I realized how my own feelings had changed. When I first saw the Facebook comments, I wanted to hide and pretend that none of them were real. I was wanting to go into the denial state when it hit me—something out of the ordinary could be done to change my feelings and possibly theirs as well. My anxiety was gone. I was no longer hurt and upset. There was relief when my attitude changed from allowing bitterness to enter my heart to having a sincere desire to show grace instead. As I look back, showing grace in that moment was the best thing I could have done. Not only did it help rid me of negative thoughts toward the women, but it also gave them a chance to visit our showroom and hopefully have an experience that was a blessing.

Recently I went with Terry and the girls to a local restaurant for dinner. I had never before experienced such poor service as I did with our waitress. That poor service, coupled with a sour disposition, could have ruined our night. My first reaction was to give her back the same snappy attitude she was dishing out to us. I was certain I'd receive some sort of satisfaction knowing she would be the recipient of her own unkindness.

> We will always encounter people who are angry
> or who might push our buttons. Usually they are
> the ones who need our kindness the most.

In that moment, however, I decided to try to look beyond her actions and her outer shell. Even though it was not easy or natural for me, I decided to shower her with kindness and engage her in conversation to find out who she was. And I truly was interested in getting to know her since I am a *people* person.

An amazing thing happened when I offered her kindness and grace! Her angry shell started to crack. She showed signs of a smile and began to relax since she didn't get the response she deserved or expected for her attitude. So during that one meal this waitress let her guard down, and I let my defenses go. The exchange between patron and server actually turned out to be enjoyable rather than an all-out war of words.

We will always encounter people who are angry or who might push our buttons. Usually they are the ones who need our kindness the most. Hurting people hurt others, but when we show kindness and grace instead of retaliation, often the barriers disappear.

When the world stands to the side and begins to judge, you be the one to look past the covers of their books, knowing they are walking in chapters that require extra grace.

You have the power to help rewrite a line in their stories with your kindness. It becomes addictive and contagious.

So look for the books that aren't open.

The ones you can barely read.

Pick up your pen.

And with God's grace help them write a new line.

Chapter 17

DREAM BIG DREAMS; THEN DREAM BIGGER

WHETHER ANYONE WANTS to admit it or not, everyone has a dream. Your dream is the thing that your heart whispers to you in the still of the night and in the busyness of the day, the thing that keeps coming back to you and ignites your soul with excitement.

The beautiful thing about dreams is that they don't have an expiration date. Many dreams have been laid down temporarily for present and pressing responsibilities. But just when you thought your quiet dream had disappeared, it finds its way back into your heart. And what you may realize is that, even though time has passed and your dream seems distant, it actually never left, and it never ended. It was simply on pause.

I can list out many dreams I have had since I was a little girl: to be an Olympic gymnast, to learn how to tap-dance like Fred Astaire, to marry Terry Donovan, to never have to shave my legs again (shallow, I know, but a dream nonetheless), to practice law with my dad, and many more. But the dream that never escaped me was to find something I am truly passionate about, to love what I do, to not dread Monday mornings. This was one dream I thought was not even possible, particularly considering I had worked so many years and never found something I was even close to being in love with.

As a little girl I faithfully watched the Miss America pageant every single year. I would write down my top ten as soon as they all came out. I didn't know any of the contestants yet was rooting for some as if they were my own family.

My favorite part was the interview portion of the pageant. It was the time when we finally got to hear the women talk and get a feel for their personalities. Watching the interviews often changed things for me, and I began rooting for the women who were relaxed, witty, and genuine—the ones I would want to hang out with or have as a big sister.

> ### The beautiful thing about dreams is that they don't have an expiration date.

While I was in college, I would push my girlfriends to ask me on-the-spot questions, as if I were competing for the title. I would pretend to be onstage, with millions watching on television, and then attempt to answer the random question given to me. For what it's worth, I think I would have gotten poor marks for saying so much yet saying nothing at all! I have since learned that less is more.

Four years ago I was given third-row seats to the entire week of the Miss Oklahoma pageant. The tickets took me by surprise, and I was interested in going since the entire production still fascinated me. During the pageant I was taken back to my childhood and didn't want to miss a single night of the preliminaries or the finals. I knew who maybe one or two of the contestants were, but otherwise I was getting to know these ladies just as I got to know Miss America contestants for years on television.

It came to me: With all the challenges, preparation, money spent, sweat, and tears these women had experienced over the previous year, it all came down to this one final night. And only one girl would go home as Miss Oklahoma.

All of them had hopes of winning the title and crown, and the winner could go on to compete in the Miss America pageant in the fall. The loss so many of these women would experience wasn't for a lack of preparation or hoping or praying. It simply came down to the fact that only one girl could win.

Since that first captivating summer there hasn't been a summer that I have missed the pageant. I have come to know and talk to some of the wonderful and talented girls who continue to pour their hearts and souls into being the best they can be each year.

This past summer, the night before the final competition, I decided to turn the tables on the forty-five contestants and ask them a very specific question, an unusual one. "Tomorrow night only one of you will go home as Miss Oklahoma. The other forty-four of you will wake up on Sunday possibly asking yourself, 'What should I do now?' Some of you may already know the answer, but some of you have not planned past tomorrow night. So here is the question I would love for you to answer: If you could wake up on Sunday morning and do one thing for yourself, one new thing that you could be intentional about for the next year, what would it be?"

Some of the girls smiled since they knew right off what their answer would be. Some of them were deep in thought. The lovely girls truly had been so focused on what they were doing that they didn't have time to look past the next night. I had not preplanned this, nor did I have any idea how the next hour was going to play out. What happened, though, was truly magical.

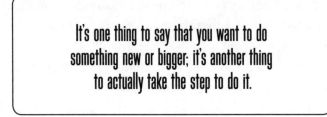

It's one thing to say that you want to do something new or bigger; it's another thing to actually take the step to do it.

It was as if all competition ceased, and the girls began to dream beyond Saturday night. They were faced with a question, and their answer could present exciting opportunities. Each one took a minute or two and shared what it was that she wanted to do if she could intentionally do something for herself starting on Sunday, the day after the finals. Watching them reflect on something outside the pageant was truly special. Hearing their hearts and listening to one another share a little bit of their desires for a new dream brought them all closer together in an unexpected way.

Their answers ranged from, "I want to learn how to play the guitar my grandpa left me when he died," to "I want to save up the money to get a great sewing machine so I can continue to learn how to sew and make things for others." It sparked something inside of me that made me want to help each girl live out her dream or goal. It's one thing to say that you want to do something new or bigger; it's another thing to actually take the step to do it.

I figured out a way to help each woman take the first step. Whether it was giving one the money to buy tap shoes for the lessons she wanted to take that year or sending another a sewing machine, we found a way to help them take the dreams beyond just words. Again, this is not something that was planned at all, yet in the end it turned out to be better than anything we could have organized or done with the forty-five girls, who were getting ready to face one of the biggest nights of their lives.

On Saturday night, as I watched all of them come out and perform for the Miss Oklahoma title, I smiled inside. Just knowing they had vocalized and possibly even put into motion a plan for something new and fun on Sunday made me much more relaxed and content for each one of them.

So as big as the dream of winning Miss Oklahoma and then moving on to Miss America is in the hearts of so many girls, "Sunday" will come for most of them. The message I wanted to tell each one was that as big as that dream to be crowned with the title seems, they can still dream even bigger. The dream doesn't end on Saturday night. Instead, it is simply an opportunity to go explore what may feel like a small dream at the moment yet has larger-than-life possibilities.

So for those of you who think you are way past the point of your dream coming to life, please think again.

Remember your dream.

Dust it off, or create a new one.

Write it down, and then take that piece of paper and turn it over. On the other side write an even bigger dream than you think is possible.

And continue to find joy in what you currently do, all the while working, thinking, praying, and pursuing that which your heart whispers to you in the still of the night.

Chapter 18

THIS TOO SHALL PASS

WHEN I WAS fourteen years old, my friends were going on a ski trip, but I was unable to join them. The upcoming trip was the main topic of conversation for weeks before they departed. I was terribly sad when they left, knowing they were making memories I'd never be part of. There was that sick feeling in my stomach that happens to me when I am really missing out on something. Oh, how I wanted that feeling to fly away as quickly as possible. When my friends returned, the same thing happened as before they left. They reminisced about all the fun times—and reminisced and reminisced.

An idea came: I picked a date and circled it on a calendar hanging next to my bed. Until that date arrived, I'd allow myself to feel the sadness and pain. Once the circled date came, I would move past those feelings. There was no science or method to choosing the particular date. I prayed and then selected a date on the calendar that felt right. Instead of masking the pain, I gave myself the freedom to fully feel the sadness during that time. Like many people, I oftentimes try to bury or suppress the sadness. We try to make the hurt go away by *rushing through the healing process*. Shoving the emotions down so they won't surface is common among the best of people.

The experience of missing "a trip of a lifetime" with my friends was simply learning ground, a preparation for significantly more difficult experiences facing me later in my life. I might have lost the fun of skiing and fellowship, but I gained much more than I lost. Ahead were to come:

- Three painful miscarriages

- Heavy empathetic emotions watching my beloved Terry go through emotional and physical pain during a battle with cancer at age twenty-one

- The loss of my dad (my best friend) to pancreatic cancer right after I got married

What I learned from the ski trip incident was time doesn't necessarily heal all wounds...completely. But I did find out raw, can't-catch-my-breath-for-the-pain feelings will pass. We won't necessarily be able to stop the storm, but we can live with the hope that we *will* survive it and it will pass.

This pain is just a chapter in our story, not the whole book. We may not forget the chapter, but we will move past it. Sometimes all we have at our disposal is the knowledge the "hurricane" will not last forever; every storm has an ending; the sun will absolutely shine again...in time.

Your method of moving forward may not be circling a date on the calendar as I did, but we *can* decide not to bury the feelings that arise during a storm, or after a loss, or even in the middle of heartache. We all can rest in the knowledge that no matter what chapter of life we are in, no matter the "emotional nausea" we are experiencing, this too shall pass; this too shall considerably lessen, considerably weaken with time. It always does.

As long as I can remember, I have been flying (on airplanes, that is). I had no fear connected with those amazing machines. If I had the slightest bit of anxiety, I'd remind myself that flying is safer than driving in a car. (I wonder how many other travelers have reminded themselves of those very words.)

And then I was flying back to Tulsa after visiting family in Atlanta for the holidays. I was in my mid-twenties, and my purse held no harmonica. Right after takeoff large clouds surrounded the plane, causing some minor turbulence, which I'd experienced on previous flights. Soon we reached an altitude that allowed for a smoother ride. I settled in my seat, opened a book, and was wonderfully relaxed. The pilot came on the speaker, but it wasn't to thank us for choosing Delta Air Lines. "Code red, code red!" were his exact words.

> **We won't necessarily be able to stop the storm, but we can live with the hope that we *will* survive it and it will pass.**

I thought, "Well, this is something new!" Never having heard "code red" before, I could only assume something was wrong. I always try to gauge others' reactions as a barometer to help me know how to react in any situation. Based on the flight attendants' reactions (they ran toward the front of the plane), I knew a code red had to be threatening. I looked at fellow passengers near me and saw they were confused and fearful.

Panic swept over me! I reached for the phone connected to the back of the seat in front of me. I swiped my credit card as fast as possible and dialed my dad. I told him that based on what the pilot said, I thought my life was about over. I was traumatized by the announcement. My dad's calming voice helped steady my breathing. A moment later the plane seemed to be turning around. Someone next to me said we might be heading back to Atlanta.

My dad overheard the person to my left and said it was a good sign. He followed up with more reassurances: "Just a few more minutes, honey, and you will be on the ground. This too shall pass." Sure enough we landed safely back in Atlanta, and I learned that "code red" was for a medical emergency. There was a man in first class who thought he might be having a heart attack, so paramedics were at the gate to tend to him.

Although I knew what had happened wasn't at all related to the airplane itself, a fear was deposited in me I'd never had before. It was probably a tiny degree of post-traumatic stress. Now I have this fear every time I fly somewhere. Before I take off on a flight, I always pray and can clearly remember my dad saying, "This too shall pass." Taking a few minutes to do that and then recalling my dad's words allows me to balance my fears with reality. I have never since heard any code reds, blues, greens, or purples.

It's so fitting that my dad's words are a comfort to me when flying, of all things. Let me tell you why. When my dad passed away, my emotions were raw. I ached deep down in the pit of my stomach and in the center of my heart. My mom wrapped her arms around me and told me something I continue to return to for comfort even now. She told me to picture a birdcage with two little doors, one on each side of the cage. One door was for the bird to fly into the cage, and the other was the exit door. The cage represents our life on the earth, and everything outside of the cage represents eternity.

> Taking a few minutes to turn to my Father in heaven and then concentrating on my dear earthly father's words allows me to balance my fears with reality.

Mom said to picture a bird flying through the door on one side. The bird flies in for a little while and one day gets to fly out the other door. She told me I'm like the little bird, which flies into the cage for a minute and then flies out the other door. Our span on the earth is *so short* compared with our lifetime in eternity.

My dad is no longer caged. He is a free bird, soaring. I am so happy for him and will be flying out to meet him one day—and it won't be on an airplane. We would do well to always remember the birdcage is not intended to be our eternal home. This life on the earth will surely pass away in but a moment. What a reunion I will have with my dad someday when we get to hug once again.

You can use the phrase "This too shall pass" daily, as it will help keep life in perspective. We can see the bigger picture as we think of that bird flying out the door into unimaginable forever freedom. His first home, the birdcage, was never his final destination.

Nor is it ours.

Chapter 19

FIND JOY IN THE JOURNEY

I T IS A Jewish tradition to name your child after a deceased relative, thereby honoring the person's memory. Since both of my
parents come from a Jewish background, they adhered to this
custom and named me after my great aunt Fanny.

They weren't sure that Jill Fanny had that certain ring they were
going for, so they used the F from her name and gave me Felice
as a middle name. Although my parents later became Christians, I
am still grateful Mom and Dad decided to follow tradition that day
over four decades ago. Felice means "happy and joyful." I believe
my parents' steps were ordered back then when naming me.

If your name is Joy, or if it means "joy," there is no guarantee
you will experience it. Joy is not something you sit around and wait
for; it is a choice. It doesn't just happen to you when all of the stars
align. How wonderful to know we can break the habit of starting
and ending our days with complaining or living in monotony by
choosing to talk about the things we are grateful for, the parts of
life that bring us joy. Joy and gratitude go hand in hand.

Red used to be my favorite color, and honestly it still is one of my go-to colors. However, sometime during the last year I had an epiphany: the color yellow simply makes my heart smile. It reminds me of the sun and reminds me of basking in the sun's warmth, even when there are storms on the horizon. So that's why the color yellow brings me joy.

> Joy is not something you sit around and wait for; it is a choice. . . . Joy and gratitude go hand in hand.

One of my favorite quotes is "Find joy in the journey." It doesn't say, "Find joy in the destination," or "Find joy when the sun is shining." You may wait a long time before you arrive at the destination or for the sun to shine. Find your yellow, the thing that brings you joy throughout the journey. And know that every sunset also has a sunrise; every dark night yields a new day.

You and I can discover the same joy in the storms that we will find in the sunshine. In fact, true joy is letting go of the fact that you may not yet be at your "destination" but are appreciating the path you are currently on regardless. We may be at a yield sign or even find ourselves staring at a stop sign, but joy is found when we can appreciate the scenery along the way.

Maybe this will help get you started:

_____ brings me joy.

Try to stay away from answers such as these:

- "The destination"
- "The last day of school"
- "Getting out of debt"
- "Getting pregnant"
- "Meeting that special someone"
- "Getting back to a fighting weight"
- "Getting my dream job"

As I was leaving for church one night, there was a cuff on my counter that said "Embrace the Journey." I felt compelled to put it on, but I didn't know why. Over the years I have learned to trust that feeling time and time again, so I found a spot to stack it with the others already on my arm.

After the service a woman came up and introduced herself. Her name was Liz, and she had a story to share with me.

Liz had been given a cuff the previous year: "Find Joy in the Journey." She wore it every day that year as her husband was dying of stage-four cancer. She continued sharing that after he died, the cuff was too painful to wear. Not wanting it to just sit in a drawer unworn, she found someone else going through a difficult time and passed the cuff on to her.

I said to Liz, "Well, this explains why I was drawn to wear this specific cuff tonight. You may not find joy in the journey at this point, but you can *embrace* it. And someday again you will find your joy." I took "Embrace the Journey" off my arm and handed it to her. This was the reason I felt prodded to wear it that night. That evening was a very simple, yet powerful, reminder to me to never ignore that little whisper.

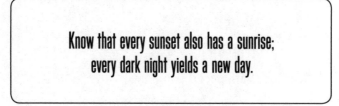

Know that every sunset also has a sunrise; every dark night yields a new day.

To Liz and all of those who struggle every day, every hour, and every minute with the heartache of missing a loved one, know that your heart will someday smile again. And until then you can embrace your journey.

DON'T COMPARE YOUR CHAPTER 1 WITH SOMEONE ELSE'S CHAPTER 20

I STARTED PLAYING TENNIS as an adult. As a beginner I was placed on the lowest-level team. There were six courts next to one another, and I could see all ranks of players. Some were on my level, and some, at the highest tier. I started comparing myself with the high-level players. I would think, "Why am I even trying this? These women are way better than I am—not to mention way younger than I am. Even if I am wearing a super cute tennis skirt!"

To stop this negative downward spiral, I decided to take my eyes off the other players and focus on my skills. My plan to stop making comparisons was to only look over to another court to learn something new. This was my own journey. I stopped talking down to myself and instead started saying, "At one point they were in my exact position—a beginner." The highly ranked players had to start somewhere too, and if they could do it, then so could I.

When Rustic Cuff first started, I was the only employee. I had no idea how big my dreams could be and had no idea what those dreams even were to begin with. I started looking around at successful people and the brands that seemed to be thriving. Seeing the Apple Facebook page, I noted the company had over one million followers. (It now has over eight million followers, so it continues full steam ahead.) When I saw it had that many followers, I immediately thought, "Well, I'm never going to get there." You see, I also had a Facebook page with followers. There were about ten people who followed my page, and those ten followers were friends and family.

As I was scrolling through the Apple Facebook page, I started thinking of ways to grow the company and realized even Apple had to start somewhere. I decided not to compare myself with that company—ever. I would not compare my current chapter to its current chapter. Rustic Cuff was only on chapter 1, while Apple was on chapter 20. For Apple to get to chapter 20, it had to start where I am now, chapter 1. Apple had to get through each chapter, 1 through 19. Additionally it's simply not a valid comparison. I was still in a canoe at this point—just trying to survive the waves in the middle of the ocean—while other people in the industry were enjoying the breeze on a yacht.

> You and I aren't meant to live someone else's story.
> We will all have our own unique story to tell.

Instead of comparison I would try to learn everything possible from successful people. I wanted to learn their mistakes and wins and to gather all the information available from the business owners who came before me.

I know someday I'll be in chapter 3, and others will be in chapter 1, and my hope is they will not compare themselves with me or anyone. I want them to know I had to get through each chapter, even with some unconventional means, before reaching chapter 3. Even today I sometimes catch myself comparing, but I have to quickly remind myself others are on their own journey as well. Everyone started out in a canoe to get to where he or she is today. There is purpose in each stage.

The key is to fully embrace the chapter we find ourselves in instead of skipping ahead. You and I aren't meant to live someone else's story. We will all have our own unique story to tell. None of us will never be fully prepared for chapter 20 until we have walked through each previous chapter. What's the point of being in a chapter we aren't equipped for? Why would we want to build anything without the proper tools? It would involve simply staring at a lot of pieces and parts with no means to put them all together. It's pivotal to soak everything we can from each line of every chapter so we are 100 percent prepared for what lies ahead in the rest of our book. I've learned I can never truly discover who God intended for me to be when I compare my journey with someone else's.

Live a life worthy of the calling and gifts you have been given. The most painful and heartbreaking experiences of our lives often are essentially linked to our purpose. It might not be the script we would have written had we penned our own story, but if it is a necessary part of the plan to which we are called...count it all priceless.

Nothing will steal the hope and joy from your heart faster than comparison.

Stay in your own story.
Continue to walk through it.
Chapter by chapter.
Not missing a single line.
Embracing every word.

Chapter 21

CULTIVATE THE HABIT
OF BEING GRATEFUL

IN ORDER TO help with law school tuition, I worked at American Airlines. After my third year of working there, a position in a different department became available, and I applied for it.

Part of the application process was to give a five-minute speech to three top executives at the company. My speech was titled "Do You See the Glass Half Empty or Half Full?" I was allowed to bring a prop, so I brought a glass of water filled exactly to the halfway point.

When I walked in to give the speech, I froze. My nerves took over, and I could not recall a single word I planned to say. I stared at the glass of water—and I knew the only way I would be able to talk would be to take a sip. "Yes," I thought. "That would help bring some clarity to the task at hand." After drinking almost all of the water in the glass, I suddenly remembered what my speech was about. Needless to say, I did not get the promotion.

I did take something away from that "memorable, yet

not-so-memorable" speech: What matters isn't whether the glass is half empty or half full but that we have glasses of water to begin with. When the glass feels half full, it's understandable that gratitude makes it overflow. But there is a benefit even to half-empty glasses because they can cause thirst. And thirst can cause us to seek and find satisfaction we otherwise might not have found.

It's not in our nature to be grateful for pain and suffering. But eventually when we look back, we will realize these bumps in the road didn't break us. They molded us. They gave us strength. Some of the "bumps" are self-inflicted because we didn't get what we wanted. There are things we think we want, and there are things we think we need in order to be happy. We tell ourselves we will be grateful when we finally get those things. However, we will probably discover those things are often not meant to be part of our stories.

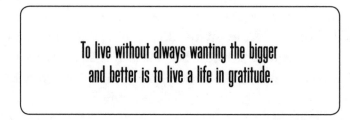

To live without always wanting the bigger
and better is to live a life in gratitude.

Showing gratitude during the hard times often doesn't make sense to our human nature. It's easy to show gratitude when the reason for the bumps becomes clear, but being grateful in the midst of pain or confusion is another story. Gratitude brings hope, and hope is a powerful thing indeed! You can choose to say, "I'm grateful for this season of waiting," or, "I'm grateful for the lesson of patience," or, "I'm grateful that God doesn't allow pain without a purpose." This attitude of thankfulness lifts us out of the mire of the moment.

To live without always wanting the bigger and better is to live a life in gratitude. Living a life in constant thanksgiving is a life filled with peace, joy, and riches that money cannot buy. The richest man in the room is truly the one who is grateful for everything he has. Let's be the one who is simply grateful for the glass, with or without much water.

It's a surreal feeling when you create something on your guest bedroom floor, and the very next week at the grocery store, on the cookie aisle, you see a stranger wearing the bracelet you created the week before.

Whenever I am out and see someone wearing a Rustic Cuff bracelet, a sense of gratitude comes over me. I want to stop her or him and say, "Thank you." I usually just smile, knowing she has no idea why I am smiling or what I am feeling inside.

Even after five and a half years of designing and creating the cuffs, I am always grateful to friends and strangers alike for wearing them. There are mornings when I turn on the television to watch a national morning show and see one of the hosts wearing one of our bracelets. I am still surprised and grateful every time.

When I first started making cuffs, at times the thought came that my family and friends felt sorry for me due to the long hours I spent creating them. I was convinced they wore the cuffs just to make me feel better. Then I noticed they kept wearing them far beyond my made-up "pity period." I don't think I will ever get used to the feeling of gratitude when I see others enjoying the cuffs.

One of our longtime Thanksgiving family traditions, before we pray over the meal, is to share what we are thankful for. I want it to be a frequent occurrence, a habit, not just a Thanksgiving tradition. Therefore, whenever we sit down together as a family for an evening meal (which is by no means as frequent as we'd like), we go around the table to share the highlight of that day and tell why we are thankful. This has a special effect on the rest of the evening because we have spoken aloud something good we found in our day that may have otherwise gone unnoticed.

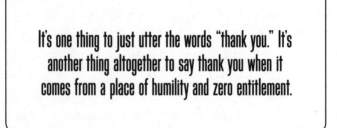

It's one thing to just utter the words "thank you." It's another thing altogether to say thank you when it comes from a place of humility and zero entitlement.

There are times someone in the Rustic Cuff family will come up and ask me, "What is something I could do for you to say thank you?" I usually answer, "You just did!" For example, Pam, a sweet girl who works in one of our Tulsa showrooms, will without fail handwrite a thank-you note every single time she receives a gift from me—for instance, an extra couple of cuffs. Within forty-eight hours that note will somehow find its way to my desk (the one I love but rarely sit at). The joy I receive from opening her cards is the type that remains with me a long time.

Being gracious and saying thank you, as Pam does so well, is a true indicator of our hearts. It's one thing to just utter the words "thank you." It's another thing altogether to say thank you when it comes from a place of humility and zero entitlement. Entitlement is one of the most unattractive human qualities. True and pure gratitude takes us out of the realm of entitlement and throws us right into the camp of humility—the only camp I want to attend.

Chapter 22

LIVE WITH INTENTION

I<small>T IS</small> so easy to just let life happen to you, rather than you happening to life.

I am the only one in my family who makes new year's resolutions, but one December I decided that needed to change. Terry, Ireland, Peanut, and I flew to Chicago for New Year's Eve so we could enjoy all the Windy City had to offer during the holiday season. (Not to mention we love negative-twenty-degree weather, so that was fun to navigate as well!)

It was a few hours before midnight on New Year's Eve, and we were all relaxing in the hotel room when I asked Terry and the girls to tell me their resolutions for the coming year. I had already written mine down in my journal (i.e., my iPhone) earlier that week, so I was all set. Terry is always reluctant to make resolutions, but he played along anyhow. Peanut told us hers, and then Ireland shocked me by saying she was completely giving up sugar. *Sugar?* In disbelief I looked at her and thought she was kidding.

Alarmed, I said, "You are my favorite sugar buddy! We are both addicted to and crave sugar like nobody else, and now you are telling me you are abandoning the sugar train? You are leaving me all alone on sugar island?"

She smiled and said, "Yes. My mind is made up. I am giving it up." And just like that it was done. Terry and Peanut care very little for sugar, so there was no hope in bringing them over to my team to play. Ireland ate her last bit of sugar before the clock struck twelve, and then with determination she gave it all up. I'm still amazed she decided to be *intentional* about something that had been such a part of our lives. We loved ice cream, snow cones, movie candy, and milkshakes. Yet she *intentionally* let it go to begin her year of driving the bus instead of letting it drive her.

> ## Decide not to *let* things happen but to *make* things happen.

I remember so many times, while eating sugar, thinking, "I'm not even hungry. I'm just eating this because it is sitting in front of me." And then my twelve-year-old daughter looked sugar in the face and said, "No thank you. I will be the one who is in charge of what I eat rather than allowing it to rule me."

What an inspiration she has been to me! Not only to watch her give up sugar but also to do it almost effortlessly. I believe it is because she actually *intended* to do this instead of saying, "Maybe I will do this if I feel like it."

The same determined focus that started on the first of January carried over to other areas of her life as well. Ireland had the confidence knowing the discipline was there. All she had to do was make a purposeful plan.

One night before bed a strange thing happened to me. I removed a stack of cuffs from my wrist, but there was one bangle I couldn't get off. I tried several times but to no avail. Never had there been an issue with this cuff before. After a minute of trying, I decided to just go to bed with the cuff on. I'd leave it be and try again tomorrow. But I need to tell you, this was odd, very odd.

The next day I met Terry for lunch and had only one cuff on my wrist—the unremovable one. (I hadn't donned additional cuffs, as I was going to a dance class before lunch and didn't want to wear them there.)

At the restaurant with Terry I ran into Maggie, an old friend I had graduated law school with. She and her family had moved away after school but had recently returned to Tulsa. Maggie confided that her family was going through a hard time, and she was struggling with a critical decision that needed to be made concerning her marriage. The situation was extremely unhealthy for her entire family, and something needed to change.

I listened with my heart and only wanted to speak words of wisdom to her. She and I began talking about options. I encouraged her to be intentional in making a decision since wavering back and forth was causing distress to her family. I offered, "I'm thinking you really want to preserve your sanity and not spend your summer living a life in limbo. Whether you decide to seek help to work it out together or whether you know it's simply not a possibility anymore, wouldn't it be better for this to be a summer of intention?" I really cared about Maggie and was hoping she'd be able to wake up every day having come one step closer to a resolution.

As we said goodbye, I looked at my wrist and decided to try one more time to undo the bangle I had struggled with the night before. To my amazement, without any trouble at all I unclasped it and looked at the quote on the cuff. This one was made just for Maggie! It read "Live with intention." I half expected her name to be engraved on the inside. Once it was off my wrist, I clasped and unclasped the cuff several times to make sure nothing was wrong with it. It was working perfectly, and I knew clearly the bracelet was not meant to come off my wrist the night before when readying for bed. I handed the quote cuff to her and said, "Here is something to serve as a reminder for you each day."

> You can be the reader of stories, or you can be the one stories are written about. It's your choice.

I saw Maggie eight weeks after her summer began (still wearing the cuff), and she told me, "Living this summer with intention was the greatest gift I could have given to my children." She went on to say she was finished with the indecisiveness and was finished with the accidental living that had trapped her for so long. Maggie still had not come to a full resolution, but she had moved much closer than she had been when we met weeks earlier. The best part: my friend had a peace and a hope that had been nonexistent before, and she was now living with purpose.

We can choose to start each day with intention. You can purpose to set new goals with intention to see them through, knowing there will be roadblocks, twists, and turns. It helps immensely to keep our plans and intentions before us in the forefront of our minds or on paper. This way they are easy to see. What Maggie and Ireland did when they decided not to *let* things happen but to *make* things happen worked wonders in their lives.

Intentionality can also include acts of kindness. We can sit back and listen all day to reports of random acts of kindness and think to ourselves, "What a great story. If only things like that happened to me." You may put this book down and think, "Someday I am going to figure out a way to do something kind for a stranger...someday." You can make it happen and begin to do it now. You can be the reader of stories, or you can be the one stories are written about. It's your choice.

PART 3
SPEAKING OFF THE CUFF

*Kindness is a language that the deaf
can hear and the blind can see.*[1]
—MARK TWAIN

Chapter 23

YOUR "KNOWER"

(Better Than a Teleprompter)

MOST PEOPLE ON television consider teleprompters invaluable for staying on track during prepared speeches. I consider the promptings of my "knower" even more invaluable. From the almost magical beginnings of Rustic Cuff to today I have depended on these promptings. I doubt the company would have been created without them.

God is my ultimate teleprompter—prodding me from within to give and impassioning me to be generous when I do. Those of us who work tirelessly at Rustic Cuff are learning to listen better to the promptings of the heart. Behind the scenes a giving attitude has been contagious from the outset.

This book was not meant to add one more responsibility to your to-do list or burden you in any way. Instead of kindness becoming a stress in our lives, we simply want to grow in our ability to sense promptings. At the beginning of the book I mentioned that the word *knower* has to do with following your heart, listening to the still, small voice within, discerning situations, and being alert to gentle, or sometimes strong, prodding. That prodding is not just a made-up idea appearing out of thin air. God placed it in your heart.

When we feel something deep within prompting us to do something for someone else, the key is to just act on it. Without over-analyzing. If we think about it long enough, we will talk ourselves right out of it. And when we act on it, let's do it wholeheartedly. Do it completely. If I feel as if I am supposed to do something specific for someone, I don't want to shortchange the person by only doing part of it and telling myself it was enough that I even did something in the first place. We all get promptings to do something for a reason—a reason that we may never know. So I have learned not to partially obey following my heart.

> That prodding is not just a made-up idea appearing out of thin air. God placed it in your heart.

In the first year of Rustic Cuff, as the empty gifting closet was beginning to fill up with handmade cuffs, I felt it was time to pull some off the shelves to gift to others. On my right wrist I always wore either cuffs that Terry had given me as special gifts or bracelets the girls had made. But on my left wrist I decided to wear cuffs I had created in that guest room in the middle of the night—these would be for giving away.

Up to this point it was not difficult to give cuffs to friends or family, as it seemed there was always a birthday or celebration around every corner. But one afternoon I sensed it was time to venture beyond my comfort zone and give a cuff to a complete stranger.

I imagined it would feel awkward to approach a woman I didn't know, remove a cuff from my arm, and offer it to her. What words should accompany that gesture? And yet I could no longer ignore the prompting to do this. It was as if this were the moment I had been preparing for all year long. But I feared discomfort. What if the person rejected my gift?

It was the end of the day, and my heels were pinching badly, making me wonder why I hadn't reached for flip-flops instead. I needed to stop for milk and eggs on the way home, and at the crowded food store I couldn't escape the feeling that this was my time. A sudden wave of anxiety came over me. Not only were my feet in pain, but I was getting ready to do something nerve-racking—this felt harder than the speech I'd given years ago when I was going for a promotion at American Airlines, when I forgot the subject entirely.

I realized that if God had given me this task, He would also provide the grace and boldness to complete it. Grabbing my carton of milk and the eggs, I headed for the checkout, only to realize most lines were four to five people deep. That is when I saw her.

Of course she'd be the cashier with the longest line.

Of course she'd be the one who wasn't smiling.

I wanted to kick off my heels and run for the car. "Did I really need the milk and eggs? Couldn't we just take the girls to get doughnuts for breakfast on the way to school instead of eating at home?" Yet as all of these thoughts were swirling through my head, I found myself at the end of her line.

You know the feeling when you have no other choice but to listen to your heart, or you will spend the next day (or week, or month, or year) wishing you had? Well, I didn't want that feeling. No thank you. I've had it before, and it wasn't worth it. This time, despite the possible embarrassment, I was not going to ignore the prompting. No sir!

By the time it was my turn to check out, there were five people in line behind me. Yes, I counted. After taking a deep breath, I smiled at the cashier and said, "Hi! I don't think we have ever met, but I wanted to give you a bracelet."

She looked straight at me, and tears filled her dark brown eyes.

Everyone began staring at her.

Then at me.

People wondered what was going on.

She began to cry as she put the cuff on. Through her tears she told me, "You would have no way of knowing this, but yesterday I was diagnosed with breast cancer. When I was given the news in my doctor's office, I prayed and asked God to just give me a sign of hope that everything was going to be OK."

Looking down, I realized the cuff I had taken off my arm was pink, the color for breast cancer awareness. She smiled and said, "Thank you. You have just given me that sign of hope I asked for."

> Be willing to be inconvenienced for a short period of time so that someone else will be impacted in ways you may never know.

I went to my car and just sat there for minutes in tears. I knew then I never wanted to ignore that voice. Ever.

And to think I almost left the store for fear of how a stranger might react to a gift given for no reason. Not only would that sweet cashier have missed out on the sign she asked for; I'd also have missed experiencing what God meant for me to incorporate into everything I did from then on.

Even though I thought that it was just about giving her a cuff, what she got was a symbol of hope. The bracelet itself was insignificant. It was the message she received by the act of being gifted something. Not only did she receive hope that day, but I learned a life lesson. I told myself, "I will be willing to be inconvenienced for a short period of time so that someone else will be impacted in ways I may never know. I will not wait for big instructions. I will pass the exam on the small ones so I will be well prepared when the bigger ones come my way." On my way home I purposed to pay more attention to the promptings of my heart. This would require growing in my listening to the still, small voice that whispers at the most unusual times.

Following this experience I knew that anyone hired to work at Rustic Cuff must also understand what it means to listen to your "knower." A couple of years ago, when I had around twenty-two employees, I decided to start off the year by giving them the opportunity to sharpen this skill. I wanted to do it in such a way that would not only touch the life of someone else but also allow my employees to be fully present and listen for that still, small voice.

I knew that I could talk to them until I was blue in the face, yet all of that would mean nothing until they could experience it on their own—from their own "knower." So during the first week in January I handed each one of them a one-hundred-dollar bill. I told them that they had ten days to give it to someone when they felt led. The only rule was that it couldn't be to a family member, and it couldn't be used for services. Not that I don't love a good mani-pedi, but that's not what this experiment was about!

One by one they began to share their stories.

And one by one we were each moved by the timing and emotions not only of the receiver of the gift but of the giver of the gift! Watching them experience irrational giving in a way that was intentional gave me so much joy that it's difficult to put into words.

> You don't have to wait until you are financially secure to give to someone else. You don't have to wait until you have all of your own emotions in check to comfort someone else's heart. Do the very best right where you are.

Each story was so moving that anyone who was nearby listening would be in tears by the time the story ended. Like this one:

One of the girls, Christine, went to the bank to make a deposit. The day was beautiful, and she decided to stretch her legs and walk into the branch instead of using the drive-through window, which was her usual habit. She was not on a mission for a special stranger to gift the money to at this time.

Christine told us she totally trusted that when the right person came along, she would know. As she stood in line, the woman in front of her caught her attention. As Christine knew would happen, the right one had "found her."

As the woman walked away from the counter and was leaving the bank, Christine got out of line and caught up to her, holding out the bill. "I think I am to give you this money."

The shocked woman immediately started crying and spilled her heart out. It was clear she really needed someone to talk to. The woman was a single mother with children waiting for her at home, and she had come to the bank to make the final installment on a bill she owed. She said she was tired of living in debt and had disciplined herself to make regular payments.

She shared that with this final payment, though, her concern was there wouldn't be money left over for groceries in the coming week. She said there was a peace about paying it off and knew deep inside that somehow God was going to take care of her.

That need was met by an overjoyed Christine, who left that day with a feeling she somehow was part of something bigger than herself—a group of people who began to irrationally give. Even when it doesn't make sense.

Especially when it doesn't make sense!

Be fully present and aware of that still, small voice.

You don't have to wait until you are financially secure to give to someone else. You don't have to wait until you have all of your own emotions in check to comfort someone else's heart. Do the very best right where you are. Even if you think the prompting is outside of your box or your current comfort level, obey that voice, and you will soon realize that the reward of gifting comes back to you in ways that exceed even your own dreams.

Chapter 24

FULL-CIRCLE MOMENT

D IFFICULT MOMENTS OFTEN come full circle in a redemp-
tive way. I experienced a full-circle moment in March 2016
when I received a letter from Oprah's company. This time
it was regarding something completely different from my experience a few years prior on the show. The letter actually started out,
"Congratulations, Jill!" The letter went on to say that Oprah would
be wearing a Rustic Cuff on the cover of *O, The Oprah Magazine*
for the month of March.

I was shocked at what I had read, and honestly I kept thinking
that someone was playing a trick on me. When I looked again in
the envelope, there was a copy of the magazine cover inside. I saw
Oprah standing with her arm on her hip, smiling as if she were
looking directly at me.

Then I noticed her wrist. And my heart smiled. I paused for a
moment just to take it in. Oprah, on the cover of her magazine,
was wearing Rustic Cuff! I want to add—I had not been in contact
with anyone at Oprah's company for years. The last time was a call

from Maria, Oprah's production assistant, letting me know when my episode would broadcast again.

I had sent a set of cuffs to Oprah recently, but the cuff she was wearing in the photograph was not one of those. Suddenly it hit me! I had gifted that particular cuff to Gayle King, Oprah's best friend. On separate occasions I had seen Gayle wearing Rustic Cuff on the CBS morning show.

God's plan is so perfect it trumps
any disappointments in life.

I am not certain that the cuff Oprah was wearing was regifted to her by Gayle or given to her by someone else, but for that moment in time, as I stood there holding the March 2016 issue, this is the story I saw. It was not one I could ever have written myself because it seemed too far-fetched. Is it possible that the circle had finally completed itself in a way only God could have orchestrated? It was a story that still continues to remind me of God's sense of humor and that He is a much better storyteller than I could ever aspire to be.

People ask quite often if I wish Oprah would put two and two together—they're referring to my being on her show years earlier and the fact that she's now wearing a Rustic Cuff that was possibly *regifted* to her. Some people have even asked if I planned to contact her and tell her the story. But seeing the cuff on the March cover and appreciating how wonderfully everything has played out—that has been more than enough for me. Oprah has done thousands of shows, and I doubt she would remember my episode. To receive the letter and the magazine's cover page was a little nod from God letting me know I was in the right place at the right moment with the right person.

I look back on the pain felt years ago on *The Oprah Winfrey Show* with complete clarity now, and I am reminded that God's plan is so perfect it trumps any disappointments in life.

Except for that pain, I would not have emptied the shelves of my gifting closet.

And but for the shelves being empty, I never would have had a burning desire to fill them again.

And but for filling them again and starting over, I may never have fully realized my passion...which led me directly to my purpose.

Chapter 25

THE KINDNESS EFFECT

B
Y THIS POINT you may be thinking, "I don't have the time,
the resources, or the energy to handle even an ounce more
than I am already handling in my own life on a daily basis."
Everything is relative, and if we each dedicate a small part of
every day to intentionally being kind to someone, we could make
a profound impact on the world. Being kind can range from something small, such as showing courtesy or giving an encouraging
word, to something larger. Each act of kindness means something
to the receiver and to the giver.

I do love all sides of Rustic Cuff, but mostly I love my employees
and the people who make up the entire family whom I get to communicate with regularly. I love knowing someone can come to one
of our showrooms to get a gift for a loved one who may be hurting
or aching from a loss, and the small act of receiving kind words on
a cuff can make a difference where sometimes nothing else seems
to be able to reach.

As cliché as it sounds, the effect of kindness is simply a ripple,
a ripple to be seen and felt so strongly it continues far beyond the

first initial act. Whether we are in the first wave of that ripple or we are starting our own ripple, we don't need much to begin. It does not require money. It only requires a bit of our heart and perhaps some creativity. Never underestimate what a simple smile can do for someone who is hurting. Your words, actions, and thoughtfulness have the power to change someone's life in ways you may never know.

You may find the effect that kindness has on your heart to be quite addicting. It releases joy and gives a high nothing else can produce. Before you know it, you start looking for ways you can answer the question "How can I change a line in someone's story from helplessness to hope?"

> The effect of kindness is simply a ripple, a ripple to be seen and felt so strongly it continues far beyond the first initial act.

You might not realize it, but your own outlook will change from looking inward to looking outward. It becomes less about *me* and more about others. Your questions are no longer:

- "What am I going to do that benefits me today?"
- "How can I manipulate this situation for my benefit?"

They are more like:

- "Whose life can I make a difference in today?"

Recently I was interviewed by a local television station, and one of the questions asked was, "What is the best thing that has come out of Rustic Cuff so far?" I answered, "Other than feeling like we are at summer camp every single day, it is simply the ability to irrationally give to others unexpectedly." Each gift creates a ripple that becomes larger as it moves outward.

I recently met two women, Amanda and Rebecca, at a Sandi Patty concert in Tulsa. Both of them were full of life and personality. I knew nothing about them, but I loved their smiles and the joy they exuded. We chatted and exchanged information. I left the concert compelled to do something fun for the girls. It took me all of two minutes to decide what I wanted to do.

I remembered Rebecca saying she was turning forty the next July and that she would like to go on this cruise to Alaska where Sandi Patty would be one of the performers. (Sandi happens to be one of my all-time favorite voices and a dear friend.)

The next morning I mailed two cuffs with anchors on them, along with a letter informing the ladies that each bracelet represented a cruise to Alaska in July with Sandi Patty—flights included. After mailing the cuffs and the letter, I walked around with the anticipation of a little girl on Christmas morning. I was not even the one who would be opening the gifts!

The two received the package and videoed the opening. After I watched the video, I can say Amanda's and Rebecca's tears of joy and excitement were nothing compared with the feeling I had viewing it. It was indescribable and a joy I want to experience over and over again. I can't wait to hear about their trip, and I'm sure my feelings will be just as strong as when I first saw the video.

I hesitated to share this story for fear that someone would think I did it for purposes less than pure. The truth is, I would not care if they told a single soul. Sometimes it is actually easier that way.

Once you experience the high of doing something completely unexpected and irrational for someone else, especially a stranger, you will start to look for ways to make a difference. Whether it is for someone who may be hurting or someone who could use a friend or a simple sign that someone actually does care, it will soon become a habit that you find yourself automatically doing on a regular basis.

When an opportunity for giving presents itself, I don't overthink; very little wavering happens. If there is a sense of peace, then I go for it. I rarely find myself asking anyone's opinion on whether or not to give in a particular situation. This has worked well so far, and I'm sticking with it!

It's best not to ask ten different people whether you should do something your heart is prompting you to do. Doing so can kill the organic nature and spontaneity of the act even before it occurs.

People often ask, "Jill, are you sure the receiver of your irrational act of kindness will receive it with the right mind-set? How will they handle it?" or "Jill, are you wondering what they're going to do with the gift or money you just gave them? Suppose what they do with it won't be to your liking."

> It's best not to ask ten different people whether you should do something your heart is prompting you to do. Doing so can kill the organic nature and spontaneity of the act even before it occurs.

The reality is that it doesn't matter. The other person's response to my gift is not my responsibility, thank God. What someone does with my kindness or gift is not up to me. My only responsibility is to follow my heart and listen to my "knower." There is really no way possible for anyone to discern the true heart of another person. Only God knows this.

You or I might give to someone who has a zero reaction. The person might even look at us as if we have lost our mind. Perhaps the act of kindness is not even appreciated at that moment. It's possible the receiver does not know the effect the gift might have on his or her future.

It is not our responsibility to know what will happen after we express an act of kindness or irrational giving. It isn't even our job to wonder what might happen. What a freedom there is in knowing it's that simple. We only need to listen and follow that prompting; the rest is God's responsibility.

A friend recently told me he and his son were sitting at a red light, and there was a man on the side of the road. He was holding a sign that read:

"Willing to work. Anything helps. God bless."

My friend reached for his wallet, took out a twenty-dollar bill, and handed it to this man. The interaction was that short—nothing extraordinary, just giving. The light turned green, and they pulled away.

> What a freedom there is in knowing it's that simple. We only need to listen and follow that prompting; the rest is God's responsibility.

The son asked, "Dad, don't you think he is just going to buy alcohol or drugs with the money you gave him?" The dad answered that beyond his obedience to do what he felt led to do, it was not his responsibility. He was moved to give to a specific person on a particular day. The rest is between the receiver and God.

The one thing I am certain of is...
    Rustic Cuff is not about the cuff.
    It never was.

     The heart of it,
     and its purpose,
     goes much deeper than selling cuffs.
     It simply has served as a venue to create a ripple.
     An unexpected ripple of kindness.
     Give what you have.
     Right where you are.
     Expect nothing in return,
     and watch what happens.

It's not possible for your life to remain the same.
The joy alone will start to affect you in ways you cannot
imagine.

NOTES

FRONT MATTER

1. A. R. Asher, accessed December 4, 2017, https://www.instagram.com /a.r.asher/?hl=en. Used with permission.

PART 2:
FOR THE LOVE OF QUOTES

1. Michel F. Bolle, *100 Inspirational Quotes* (Hamburg, Germany: Tredition, 2017), 7.

CHAPTER 9:
BE FEARLESS IN THE PURSUIT
OF WHAT SETS YOUR SOUL ON FIRE

1. Jessica Durando, "15 of Nelson Mandela's Best Quotes," *USA Today*, December 5, 2013, https://www.usatoday.com/story/news/nation -now/2013/12/05/nelson-mandela-quotes/3775255/.

2. "C. S. Lewis Quotes," Goodreads, accessed October 30, 2017, https:// www.goodreads.com/quotes/812245-you-are-never-too-old-to-set -another-goal-or.

CHAPTER 10:
KINDNESS IS ITS OWN LANGUAGE—
STUDY IT UNTIL YOU ARE FLUENT

1. Gary Chapman, *The Five Love Languages* (Chicago, IL: Northfield, 1995).

CHAPTER 14:
FAITH IN GOD INCLUDES FAITH IN HIS TIMING

1. Corrie ten Boom, *Tramp for the Lord: The Story that Begins Where the Hiding Place Ends* (Fort Washington, PA: CLC Publications, 1974), 12.

PART 3:
SPEAKING OFF THE CUFF

1. Mark Twain Center for Studies, accessed October 31, 2017, http:// marktwainstudies.com/apocryphaltwainoptimism/.